STUDENT ALIENATION
and dissent

Critical Issues in Canadian Education Series

Alan J. C. King, Editor

STUDENT ALIENATION
and dissent

Joel O. Loken

Faculty of Education

Queen's University

P
h

Prentice-Hall ♣ of Canada Ltd.

Scarborough   Ontario

PRENTICE-HALL, INC., ENGLEWOOD CLIFFS, NEW JERSEY
PRENTICE-HALL INTERNATIONAL, INC., LONDON
PRENTICE-HALL OF AUSTRALIA, PTY., LTD., SYDNEY
PRENTICE-HALL OF INDIA PVT., LTD., NEW DELHI
PRENTICE-HALL OF JAPAN, INC., TOKYO

Library of Congress Catalog Card No. 73–2168

ISBN
0–13–855742–X (pa.)
0–13–855759–4 (cl.)

1 2 3 4 5   77 76 75 74 73

PRINTED IN CANADA

To my parents,

*whose values and attitudes contrasted sufficiently
with their social milieu that their children were
able to compare at least two ways of living*

Contents

Illustrations

Tables

Series Editor's Preface

THIS SERIES of books is designed primarily for practising educators and teachers-in-training. Nevertheless, anyone concerned with serious inquiry into the educational process in Canada should find each volume a stimulating learning experience. The authors, experts in their own educational fields, have been encouraged to put forth their unique points of view and scholarship in discussions of key Canadian educational issues. Themes as diverse as the impact of the counterculture, the role of media and technology, educational equality, change and innovation in the schools, and religion have been included.

While the volumes focus on the implications of various factors for learning in schools, an attempt has been made to demonstrate the interrelationships between the economy, politics, major social trends, and education. Each issue is presented within a historical framework and then developed in a contemporary context. The format allows instructors to use the volumes individually or in various combinations depending on the nature of the courses they offer. The main purpose of the series is to broaden the perspective of the practising educator so that he can more effectively meet the challenge of educating our young.

ALAN J. C. KING

Preface

A PURELY OBJECTIVE approach requires that the sociologist refrain from allowing personal perceptions to influence what he sees. However, Carl Weinberg, in *Humanistic Foundations of Education*, has suggested that "in order to see any humanistic possibilities in sociology or in sociological study of the school, we need to reject both the necessity, and the possibility, that the sociologist exist as a true scientist." Humanistic sociology accepts some of the dangers of a value commitment, "for it prefers the risk of ending in distortion to beginning in it" (Alvin W. Gouldner, *The Coming Crisis of Western Sociology*). Perhaps it is fair to say that when one is a sociologist he should try to be objective, but when one is a humanist it is more difficult to be objective. A humanistic sociologist treads an uneasy path between analysis and apologetics.

In the first chapter a typology is provided which allows the reader to identify two dominant groups of dissident students within the high school: alienated students and students actively committed to change. Two student subcultures are dealt with which seem to have values opposed to values within the dominant culture. The emphasis in the following chapters is on the nature of student opposition and the points of disjunction between students, both alienated and dissenting, and their educators.

Educators take varying positions in responding to problems created by disenchanted students. These educator responses are systematized into different philosophical positions in the final chapter.

The author is aware that in drawing attention to student grievances the status quo may be challenged. By identifying and describing new forces, change is sometimes promoted. New alternatives for educational organization should unfold in the light of demands placed upon education by its clients—the students.

JOEL O. LOKEN

STUDENT ALIENATION
and dissent

1 Introduction to student disaffection

Before a subculture within a larger social system can be analysed, its general place within that system must be specified. A subculture within a larger culture is identifiable only in reference to that with which it is compared and contrasted. It is the purpose of this book to identify and to describe dissident student subcultures that are increasingly evident within the modern high school.

BEFORE A GENERAL typology of student groupings can be constructed, some criterion for categorization within the system must be specified. The choice of this criterion hinges on the perspective of the social scientists. One traditional method of describing the differences between the constituent parts of a social system has been to differentiate among the members of that system on the basis of social class. Another means of categorizing individual members of any system is to examine their political role and position within that system. For instance, in political systems there are explicit differences between rule makers, administrators of the rules, and rule benefactors. In traditional, hierarchical school systems there has been a minimum of overlap between the roles of rule makers and the rule benefactors. Since education is a provincial matter in Canada, the provincial departments of education and the local school boards participate in the formation and implementation of policies. Although influenced by many pressure groups, policy makers exert more political power than do other groups in the system. The administration and staff of most public schools implement and carry out the policies established by the provincial departments of education and the school boards. Usually, students do not participate in the policy-making activity. However, they are the benefactors of the policy. Students show varying degrees of acceptance or rejection of the policies carried out in the system. It is this acceptance or rejection that enables us to differentiate between various political subgroupings of students.

3

Table 1 presents a typology of students. The typology is based upon students' acceptance (+) or rejection (−) of the goals which dominant society would have them accept, the acceptance of legitimate versus illegitimate means of attaining those goals, and the manner (active vs. passive) in which students behave in society, including their in-school activity.

Conformist students (subcultures 1 and 2, Table 1) may feel that the system itself should not be fundamentally changed. Conformist students are defined as those who tend to accept the rules and regulations of the system as they are laid down by the authorities. Conformist students constitute a majority of the student population and tend to

Table 1.   Typology of Student Subcultures

	Goals (dominant society)	Means (legitimate)	Activity vs. Passivity	Student Types
Dominant Culture				
1	+	+	active	Enthusiastic conformists
2	+	+	passive	Quiet conformists
3	+	−	active	Radical reactionaries
4	+	−	active or passive	Delinquents
Counterculture				
5	−	+	active	Active reformists
6	−	−	active	Radical leftists
7	−	+	passive	Passive critics
8	−	−	passive	Alienated students

affirm the major norms, values, and goals of dominant society. Living in a conjugal family and owning a home are examples of norms in the dominant culture of Canada. "Deferred gratification," which refers to the tendency of many people to postpone gratification in the present in order to obtain future goals, is an example of a value commonly held in middle class, white Anglo-Saxon society. The goals of obtaining a well-paying job and eventually becoming married are also examples of common goals in dominant society.

The goals of dominant society are not necessarily rejected by radical reactionary students (subculture 3) or by delinquent students (subculture 4) who may value the attainment of goals accepted by the dominant society. Delinquent students, for instance, may employ unusual means of obtaining the goals which dominant society deems worthwhile, but they do, nevertheless, accept the goals, especially the material goals. Delinquent students are characterized by their anti-system, anti-legal, and anti-social behavior, and they frequently express their opposition through aggression, violence, and rule-breaking activity. Exclusion from political life, poor social conditions, economic difficulties, or lack of legitimate opportunity are some of the factors which criminologists have identified as being antecedents of delinquent behavior. Delinquents are considered by sociologists to be a "deviant" subculture, but it can be argued, from a certain perspective, that delinquents are politically similar to the conformist subcultures. Delinquents, like the conformists, seek many of the same personal and social goals, tend to vote for conservative candidates in elections, and tend to support authority-based political systems. Delinquent students and many conformist students are similar in other respects. For instance, research conducted on a sample of young people who visited youth hostels indicated that delinquents and conformists are prone to using alcohol rather than drugs for personal and social purposes. On the other hand, radical leftist, active reformist, and alienated students are more disposed to employing drugs in order to achieve their "highs."[1]

Student subcultures collectively conceived as part of the counterculture (subcultures 5–8, Table 1) are so conceived because of their fundamental rejection of many personal and social goals, the value of whose attainment is not questioned by those in the dominant society (subcultures 1–4). The counterculture is characterized by its stated anti-materialism, its sectarian, as opposed to secular, approach to reform, and its opposition to technology and industrial production, which are dominated by the profit motive. The patterns of family life and social interaction within the counterculture are much at variance with the prevailing patterns existing in dominant society.

The counterculture is composed of active reformists and radical leftists (subcultures 5 and 6, Table 1) who openly advocate change in existing social and institutional structures, and passive critics and alienated students (subcultures 7 and 8) who ignore or take no interest in social change. Alienated students are characterized by a certain cynicism concerning the possibility of humanistic reform.[2] Activists, on the other hand, believe that change can come about if the appropriate methods are employed. However, radical student leftists believe that the changes required are so great and resistance to change is so effective that extra-parliamentary methods are probably necessary in order to bring change about. Student activists frequently demand political rights and powers in the present and reject the more established channels of expressing themselves in the school. This rejection is based upon their opinion that traditional political devices are often too cumbersome and ineffective.

Some radicals are "nihilists" or delinquent-prone activists who are all too willing to employ destructive devices in order to express their political views. Nihilism has been described by John S. Campsie as a creed based upon the repudiation of authority and the destruction of institutions that embody authority.[3] Nihilism is sometimes conceived as an anti-creed since it rejects systems of belief and every principle of value in its assertion of the sovereign freedom of the individual. Some high school "anarchists" might also fit this description. Educators must not ignore the fact that some nihilists and anarchists will be among the countercultural forces that demand change in the schools. Examples of radical activists who advocate destructive disruption of dominant society include extremists and militants of the more violent kind.

Colloquial or idiomatic terms have been used, on occasion, to describe the various types of students falling into the political sub-groupings presented in Table 1. The alienated have been referred to as "heads" or "cop-outs." The radical leftists are sometimes known as student revolutionaries or student "guerrillas." Conformist students are called "straights" by their not-so-conservative peers. These terms, how-ever, are by no means synonymous and most of the labels defy specific definition. In order not to be redundant, this book will deal mainly with alienated students (subculture 8), and radical leftist students (sub-culture 6), who constitute a sizable part of the most obviously dissident section of the secondary school student population.

Many educators have expressed the opinion that student dissenters will never be powerful and eminent enough to command the attention of the administrators and officials of the school system. The reasons given for this opinion are that the great majority of students are still acquiescent; the political radicals are easily identified, isolated, and sup-pressed; it is much easier to quit than fight; the in-high-school life of the radical is normally less than three years, giving little chance of building up continuous leadership; although students have the ability to provide an accurate critique of the high school, they are most often unable to provide convincing alternatives. In spite of the fact that some educators believe student dissent is ineffective, it is still worth while to consider the alienated and radical activist positions because much can be learned as educators consider changes in the present school system.

MODEL FOR LOGICAL ANALYSIS OF STUDENT BEHAVIOR

A logical model (Table 2) may assist in organizing discussion and analysis of behaviors such as student alienation and dissent. Discussion of these behaviors in the book follows on the pattern of a three-stage model:

● First, it is essential that the behaviors one is considering have actual referents which can be defined and observed.

- After specifying the referent, the next step is to try to determine some of the sociological and psychological antecedents of the behavior.

- Finally, it is useful to examine some of the most significant social consequents of the behavior, particularly, in this case, as those consequents affect learning, teaching, and the educational system as a whole.

Table 2. Model for Analysis of Social Behavior

Antecedents	*Referents*	*Consequents*
1 Historical—sociological	Student alienation (defined in Chap. 2)	Social (effect on society) e.g. Student-system disturbances (Chap. 4)
2 Psychological	Student dissent (defined in Chap. 3)	e.g. Educator responses (Chap. 5)
3 Interaction effects		Psychological (effect on the individual)

THEORIES ON EMERGENCE OF THE STUDENT COUNTERCULTURE

One theory has it that student dissent in the high schools is an aftermath of the political activism which took place in the universities during the 1960s. If this were so, it would be appropriate at the outset to trace the development of these protest movements from their inception up to the point at which they infiltrated the secondary school system. The university has not had a great deal of influence in creating a counterculture within the high schools. However, one fact should be apparent to those who analyse the historical development of the counterculture: as a result of developments in the universities, educators should certainly be circumspect in their approach to any dissident forces now beginning to develop in the public schools.

Those sociologists who have felt that the student rebellion filtered down into the high schools from the colleges and universities should have realized that relations between Canadian universities and high schools have never been particularly strong. A smaller proportion of students go to university after high school in Canada than in the United States. There are indications that this proportion may be even smaller in the future. Canadian universities report that a smaller percentage of high school graduates showed up for classes in the fall of 1972 than was predicted.

Grievances of the high schoolers centre on personal problems regarding their own difficulties and immediate liberation from authority.

University dissent focusses more on issues relating to national and international problems removed from the personal area of gaining one's own autonomy within a system. However, when high school protest is compared with the student protest movement in the universities, it is usually noted that the youngsters are in some respects more radical than their university compatriots. The language of the counterculture frequently emerges first among the teen-agers. Sometimes the willingness to act in a radical manner is more characteristic of the high school protester than of the university protester. An example of this was seen at a meeting of the Edmonton Youth Movement on the University of Alberta campus where radical tactics were being discussed. The younger students appeared to be teaching the university students about revolutionary guerrilla methods and self-protection, such as posture to be utilized when faced with Mace, tear gas, and police weapons. Even if such knowledge was not particularly practical in Edmonton, knowledge of these things appeared to be almost exclusive to the younger students. The Free Speech Movement (FSM), which began in the United States and influenced many Canadian universities, did not have much effect on the Canadian high school. Students for a Democratic University (SDU), the Canadian version of Students for a Democratic Society in the United States, had only a slight short-term impact on the secondary schools in Canada.

When university activism was at its peak, certain spokesmen for radical organizations on campus were invited to speak to the high schools. However, these contacts were explicitly discouraged by school boards and principals who kept a watchful eye on potential troublemakers. Time and time again attempts were made to distribute literature such as Jerry Farber's *Student as Nigger* in the corridors and schoolyards of high schools. The unwelcome intruders were usually caught and forced to retreat with their handouts. All of these factors mitigated against the infiltration of high schools by radicals whose presence was often motivated by bitter recollections of preuniversity education.

HISTORY OF THE STUDENT MOVEMENT

Good documentaries have now been published on the historical development of student protest movements in Canada and elsewhere. Roussopoulos has edited a book entitled *The New Left in Canada.* Other good documentaries include Teodori's *The New Left: A Documentary History.* In addition, the *Journal of Social Issues* has published an entire issue on the New Left and the Old. Some may wish to consult Lewis Feuer's paper, "Patterns in the History of Student Movements." In an effort to provide the counterculture with its own eschatology, Roszak has written *Where the Wasteland Ends.*[4] These fine references render it unnecessary for another researcher to trace the historical emergence of the counterculture throughout all its antecedent movements. The overall purpose of this book is not to provide another history of the student rebellion, but rather to interpret the meaning of its present existence to educators who are concerned about its potential influence in the high school. Nevertheless a very brief sketch of some of the most significant developments in the history of the student movement may be useful in refreshing our memories.

Students have always been able to rebel in certain ways. Now, more than ever before, they have found it possible to criticize antiquated rules, irrelevant curricula, obsolete methods of teaching, and their lack of freedom and underrepresentation on policy-making bodies. Unfortunately, part of the movement to change society, universities, and schools took on a rather ugly dimension. This ugliness was characteristic of what some have termed the "hard revolution." Hard revolutionaries did such things as planting bombs and occupying buildings. Society seems to have grown tired of terrorist activities perpetrated by groups such as the Weathermen and the Front Liberation Quebec (FLQ). Many of these groups appear to have modified their methods, and terrorist groups seem less active in recent years. Some people feel that hard radicalism will completely disappear. Most Canadians have been aware of a lull in terrorist activities in Canada since the imposition of the War Measures Act in 1970, but there is some evidence to suggest that the firmly committed hard revolutionaries are regrouping and re-entrenching for future confrontation. Student demonstrations over various issues began cropping up again in Canadian schools and universities in late 1972.

Meanwhile many young people seem to be rethinking their basic philosophies and value orientations. Some have learned from bitter experience that hard revolution may not be the best way to achieve constructive outcomes. One reality faced by student dissidents is the existence of counter-revolutionary and reactionary forces which are more willing to act than the students anticipated. Because of these forces, certain forms of aggressive revolt have ceased to be effective means of combatting "the Establishment." Uncoordinated and chaotic attacks by various groups of students have not matched the more unified counter-revolutionary front presented by the system. More recently the protest movement has shifted from advocating a political revolution to "living" a cultural and educational revolution.

Some of the older protest groups such as the Yippie movement lacked credibility and political strength. This was understandable in that the Yippie movement, or Youth International Party, was designed as a nonorganization, and was intended to be a nonpolitical party. Jerry Rubin, author of *Do It!* and one of the Chicago Seven, thought that the myth of the Yippies would overthrow the government, but this dream itself was mythical. The Yippies' basic statement of policy was a blank sheet of paper. The Yippie rebellion was channelled into a dope/rock music be-in. Rubin screamed, "Live the revolution and screw the system." The Yippies thought that their collective energy in one place at one time would turn on the world, that it would be the "atom bomb" explosion of the youth culture. The problem with the Yippies was that, while they were claiming people should get together, they were holding demonstrations about nothing—nothing was being represented and little was being done.

Jimi Hendrix, the father of Narcotic Fantasia imagery, felt that change in the world would come through music, and he developed a form of music designed to blow people's minds. He used outer-space imagery and powerful "dope music." Rock music had converted the souls of the youth to drugs, trip fantasia, love, and peace; drugs deepened the disorienting effects of the music, and political ends were left far behind. Wishful dreaming and desiring to "return to the Garden" took over. Joni Mitchell dreamed she saw "bombers in the sky turn into butterflies over our nation."

The Monterey Pop Festival and Woodstock brought all the forces together—acid dancing, screaming, and uniting on all levels with everyone; rock music was the medium which may have brought the counterculture together. One irony, however, was that the musicians, once seen as part of the revolution, were paid exorbitant sums to perform at the pop festivals. The participants soon found that it was the dollar, rather than the revolutionary ideals, which controlled the festivals. The media then linked LSD to chromosomal damage, which moved the counterculture away from the number one "mind tripper." Grass was illegal, expensive, and hard to get. The youth culture turned to speed and heroin, and thousands died of overdoses.

The winter of 1971 experienced a recession, a calm in the youth revolution; however, its cultural influence had changed and energized the country. The larger society had adopted many of the trappings of radicalism. Capitalists had taken control of the rock industry long before 1971. There developed almost a legal tolerance for marijuana. Long hair became symbolic of fashion, not revolution.

The winter of 1971 evidenced a reassessment in radical tactics. Time out was called to organize, to call political rallies and demonstrations. Revolution had changed from a strategy for social change to a cult in its own justification. According to Herbert Marcuse, the "Prophet of the New Left," a whole re-examination of the strategy of the movement was required. This re-examination occurred. Some radicals began to believe that the population had to be radicalized through education. Revolution had to take place through more traditional means.

The tight economic situation in America began to dictate new concerns for the students. The middle class rebel lost his economic security.

Jobs were scarce and money was tight. The student could no longer afford to reflect upon the future of society as a whole since his immediate welfare was more pressing.

American youth in general have been turning away from the hard acid rock, drug, love trip scene of the previous few years. Tripping out on hard drugs and rock does not seem to have provided youth with any solutions. John Lennon stated "the dream is over, the generation thing is done, we must get back to reality. Woodstock was a dream, a once-in-a-lifetime happening." Acid trips proved suicidal, not inspirational, and the deaths of Janis Joplin and Jimi Hendrix, prophets of the peace-pop festival generation, brought the movement to much needed reappraisal. Youth began to want revelations, not revolutions—a change in the value structure to peace and love. The trend turned to finding out about oneself—a search for individual understanding and for reality.

Popular music developed a concern with style and form. It became introspective. The song writers wrote about themselves, about their own "head problems." The tone was simple, pastoral, and religious, exploring elemental imagery; for example, James Taylor's "Fire and Rain" alluded to darkness and sunlight, roads travelled and untravelled, and to fears of man left unspoken. The counterculture shaped by rock music has also become more mystical and self-oriented. Young people appear to be searching for unity and organization and for a means of achieving basic understanding and communication.

Daniel Yankelovich stated that naturalism, more than music, drugs, violence, or activism, has become the focal emphasis in the student-led cultural revolution which society is now experiencing.[5] What is regarded as natural is that which is not seen as opposed to nature. The new naturalists reject the familiar idea of man's mastery over nature. The counterculture is increasingly emphasizing the importance of living close to nature and preserving the natural environment. The new naturalists emphasize looking and feeling natural (no cosmetics, no bras, no hair grooming); nonverbal expression; discovery of one's natural self; and community rather than individualistic and competitive goals. Students today tend to reject societal mores and rules which are seen to interfere with natural expression. Also rejected are "official" rather than natural forms of authority. Nuclear families no longer live by themselves in privately owned dwellings. People who feel like living together develop their own communal families. The new naturalists value sensory experience more than conceptual knowledge. Science is de-emphasized, while the mystical, unknown, and mysterious elements of nature are celebrated.

Youth of today are involving themselves in movements such as yoga, Zen, bio-energetics, autogenic training, chanting groups, group encounter, gestalt therapy, various sorts of meditation, progressive relaxation, psychosynthesis, and transpersonal association. The focus in these subcultures is on personal and interpersonal growth rather than upon resistance, confrontation, and activism. It is speculated that as disillusionment about political cures for social problems increases, and as those social problems intensify, the young will turn more and more to movements that attempt to cultivate and conserve psychic as well as physical energy.

An assortment of films have now been produced which build up and draw attention to youth's resistance to domination by authority. *The Strawberry Statement, Zabrieski Point, Easy Rider,* and *Billy Jack* were examples of movies having to do with the dissent of youth. *Billy Jack* was a great success in Canadian theatres, especially in the small towns. Television, with its entertainment dramas, such as "Storefront Lawyers," and its new shows—CBC's "Weekend" and other programs providing social information and emphasizing social injustice—has had a great effect on the minds of students in the schools.

Growing numbers of unemployed students have supplemented the previous forces of dissent in demanding change. Added to this has been a feeling among students that school conditions are increasingly deplorable. The most common complaint made by the students is that official school curricula are irrelevant. For example, in Alberta some high schools still teach ancient history to many grade ten vocational students who plan to spend only two more years at their formal education. Even some of the "technical" or "occupational" courses taken by these students prepare them for jobs already eliminated or in the process of being phased out.

Erosion in the power and authority of the principal's office has led to an overall situation regarded by many parents and taxpayers as chaos. Some feel that this situation has been purposefully initiated by more liberal educators who were experimenting with free schools, open-concept schools, and other types of educational innovation. One marked trend was the generally increased student participation in such activities as "national skip day." Teachers and administrators have become discouraged in some centres by increased pressures mounted by students.

The penalty for smoking in one Toronto high school is loss of the student identification card, which is recoverable only after explanations and apologies are offered in the vice-principal's office. A student teacher attempting to adhere to the letter of the law felt constrained to collect over sixty identification cards while visiting the washroom during a class break. Obviously, the penalty was not carrying much weight as a deterrent to the forbidden behavior.

A bewildered vice-principal in Ottawa had a file on known drug use within his school. The number of violations had increased ten times during the previous year. He continued to enforce the usual procedures of punishment, even though he knew that it was unfair to punish a few for an offence that was so widespread. He was asked how many students were implicated in the drug problem. He replied "ninety-nine percent!" His problems were intensified by the fact that the principal was off in Florida recovering from a heart attack. Such deterioration of "authority" has obviously done nothing to enhance the position of the administrators in the eyes of the students or the general public.

OTHER CAUSES OF STUDENT UNREST

In examining the possible causes for increasing student disaffection within the high schools, another hypothesis may be in order. The rising tide of high school dissent may be related to a general increase in the awareness of today's teen-ager. This phenomenon may be viewed as one aspect of a broader movement which has been termed "the revolution of rising expectations."

The revolution of rising expectations is phraseology used mainly by political scientists to describe one stage in the emergence of formerly oppressed peoples. The revolution of rising expectations occurs when the oppressed group receives information about its disadvantageous social, political, and economic position. For instance, the oppressed group may begin to experience increased prosperity as a result of political manoeuvrings. This new prosperity automatically gives the oppressed group some new power. It is the taste of a better life to come that drives the emergent people on to revolution. The implication of this theory as it applies to education is that, once the kids begin to realize that liberation is possible, they become all the more adamant in making demands upon the system that had been oppressing them.

The general drift of society is probably more responsible than the school for causing the emergence of student rebellion. Roszak blames the "technocracy" for alienating the young.[6] Roszak declares that those who govern the technocracy justify themselves by an appeal to technical experts who justify themselves, in turn, by an appeal to scientific knowledge beyond which there is no appeal. The technocracy rests on three basic premises:

- The vital needs of man are technical. If the problem does not have a technical solution it is only an illusion.
- The requisites of human fulfilment have almost been satisfied. If we are unhappy, it is only through some misunderstanding, which can be reasoned out.
- The experts, who really know the score, are all on the office payroll of the state, and/or corporate structure. With this leadership, the state can claim omniscience over its subject, by the monopoly of the experts. The advantaged minorities are assimilated by the technocracy's "absorbent power," that is, its capacity to provide satisfactions in a way that generates submission and weakens the strength of protest. The individual's primary responsibilities to his

career, social position, and the system are controlled by public relations experts who paint parodies of freedom, joy, and fulfilment which are attainable by no one other than the elite.

Many students provide opposition to this technocracy which has generally demanded conformity from the drifting middle class youth. Many youths have determined that they have no desire to become part of the rigidity and hypocrisy which appear characteristic of adulthood within this technocracy. Since schools educate people in the technical expertise necessary for operation of the technical structure, making trouble in the school is one way of fighting against the system.

Youth today are improvising their own ideals of adulthood. The resulting life styles that they engage in are very exasperating for the older generation, but youthful dissenters are probably the most effective element of society in combatting those forces which seek to depersonalize them.

In improving the educational atmosphere of today's schools, policy makers, administrators, and teachers must keep in mind the students' fundamental concerns. One major concern of the graduating student is to find satisfactory work. In the meantime students, facing the prospects of lengthy periods in school, need more meaningful involvement and responsibility in both their curricular and extracurricular activities. If the school refuses to deal with these issues, it will surely continue to alienate its students. Schools have sometimes acted as rigid and unyielding remnants of a world that has largely disappeared. The curricula that schools advance may be only a master plan of a technocracy which does not understand the genuine human needs of people. Thus, schools have functioned to maintain the status quo rather than to innovate. The main function of schools should be to enable students to develop meaningful goals and prepare them to meet those goals.

SUMMARY

The student movement, which began in the universities during the 1960s, was probably part of a larger worldwide uprising and revolution of underprivileged people. In its beginnings, the student movement was angry and militant. Later it became less militant and political, and more cultural. A word which has been used to cover a wide variety of protest movements is the term *counterculture*. The student counterculture seems to have had a significant impact upon the high school. School authorities have been trying to respond to demands placed upon the school system by the counterculture. However, it has been difficult for educators to understand and predict the meaning and the potential power of the student movement together with the drastic changes in student attitudes during the past fifteen years.

NOTES

1. Joel Loken, "Drug Use among Transient Youth," study conducted under an Opportunities for Youth grant, 1972.

2. Kenneth Keniston, *The Uncommitted: Alienated Youth in American Society* (New York: Harcourt, Brace & World, 1965).

3. John S. Campsie, *Conflict and Cooperation: An Introduction to Some Problems of International Relations in the Twentieth Century* (Toronto: J. M. Dent & Sons, 1967), p. 41.

4. Dimitrios J. Roussopoulos, ed., *The New Left in Canada* (Montreal: Our Generation Press, 1970); Massimo Teodori, ed., *The New Left: A Documentary History* (New York: Bobbs-Merrill, 1969); The New Left and the Old, *Journal of Social Issues*, vol. 27, no. 1, 1971 (entire issue); Lewis Feuer, "Patterns in the History of Student Movements," unpublished paper, Berkeley, Calif., 1965; and Theodore Roszak, *Where the Wasteland Ends: Politics and Transcendence in Post-Industrial Society* (Garden City, N.Y.: Doubleday & Co., 1972).

5. Daniel Yankelovich, "The New Naturalism," *Saturday Review*, April 1, 1972, pp. 32–37.

6. Theodore Roszak, *The Making of a Counter Culture* (Garden City, N.Y.: Doubleday Anchor Press, 1969).

BIBLIOGRAPHY

Arendt, Hannah. *On Revolution*. New York: Viking Press, 1963.

Armstrong, Gregory, ed. *Protest: Man against Society*. Toronto: Bantam Books, 1969.

Canton, Norman F. *The Age of Protest: Dissent and Rebellion in the Twentieth Century*. New York: Hawthorn Books, 1969.

Cloward, Richard A., and Lloyd E. Ohlin. "Differential Opportunity Structure." In *Delinquency and Opportunity*. New York: Free Press, 1961.

Cockburn, Alexander, and Robin Blackburn. *Student Power: Problems, Diagnosis, Action*. Baltimore: Penguin Books, 1969.

Cottle, Thomas J. *Times Children: Impressions of Youth*. Boston: Little & Brown, 1971.

Farber, Jerry. "The Student as Nigger." *This Magazine Is About Schools*, vol. 2, Winter 1968.

Gouldner, Alvin W. *The Coming Crisis of Western Sociology*. New York: Basic Books, 1970.

Gusfield, Joseph R. *Protest, Reform and Revolt: A Reader in Social Movements*. Toronto: John Wiley, 1970.

Hoffman, Abbie. *Revolution for the Hell of It.* New York: Pocket Books, 1970.

Jacobs, Paul, and Saul Landau. *The New Radicals: A Report with Documents.* New York: Bantam Books, 1966.

Lipset, Seymour Martin. *Political Man: The Social Bases of Politics.* Garden City, N.Y.: Doubleday, 1960.

Loken, Joel. "Some Correlates of Alienation." Master's thesis, University of Calgary, 1968.

————. "A Multivariate Analysis of Student Activism." Ph.D. dissertation, University of Alberta, 1970.

Long, Priscilla, ed. *The New Left: A Collection of Essays.* Boston: Porter Sargent, 1969.

McGuigan, Gerald F. *Student Protest.* Toronto: Methuen, 1968.

Newfield, Jack. *A Prophetic Minority: The Classic Definitive Study of the New Left and the Emerging Radicalism of the 1970s.* New York: Signet Books, 1969.

Quarter, Jack. *The Student Movement of the 60s.* Toronto: Ontario Institute for Studies in Education, 1972.

Rapson, Richard L. *The Cult of Youth in Middle-Class America.* Boston: Heath, 1971.

Reich, Charles A. *The Greening of America.* Toronto: Bantam Books, 1971.

Reid, Tim and Julyan. *Student Power and the Canadian Campus.* Toronto: Peter Martin, 1969.

Rubin, Jerry. *Do It! Scenarios of the Revolution.* New York: Ballantine Books, 1970.

Taube, Eva, ed. *Man in Revolt: An Anthology of Prose for Secondary Schools.* Toronto/Montreal: McClelland & Stewart, 1970.

Wallerstein, Immanuel, and Paul Starr, eds. *The Liberal University under Attack.* The University Crisis Reader, vol. 1. New York: Vintage Books, 1971.

————. *Confrontation and Counter Attack.* The University Crisis Reader, vol. 2. New York: Vintage Books, 1971.

Weinberg, Carl. "The School, the Society, and the Individual." In *Humanistic Foundations of Education.* Englewood Cliffs, N.J.: Prentice-Hall, 1972.

Westhues, Kenneth. *Society's Shadow: Studies in the Sociology of Counterculture.* Toronto: McGraw-Hill Ryerson, 1972.

2 Student alienation

To determine how many students are alienated from their school situations, the social scientist requires some index of alienation. Several measures may suffice in indicating the extent of student alienation, one of which is a study of comparative statistics on percentages of students dropping out of school. Educators are disturbed about high drop-out rates from Canadian secondary schools in the past few years, and principals tell us these rates have been increasing rapidly since 1969. The Ministry of Education in Ontario is concerned about the trend, but up to the present time it has not made the actual statistics public. However, by studying the drop-out rates in some schools, social scientists have determined that the number of school drop-outs is increasing at a significant pace in the early 1970s.

ANOTHER METHOD of studying student alienation is to examine the behavior of students who are still in attendance at school. Freeze and Armstrong are using this approach in a research project designed to determine the effects of school environment on student alienation. On the assumption that one state of mind resulting from in-school student alienation is boredom, Freeze and Armstrong examined student behaviors that were indicative of boredom. First, they established general categories of behavior which included specific student actions indicating boredom. For instance, one category of student response to boring lessons is student avoidance. Freeze and Armstrong, working at Queen's University, noticed several kinds of student-avoidance behaviors. Students may try to avoid having the teacher ask them questions by attempting to remain inconspicuous. Other students develop methods of avoiding the teacher's questions by causing him/her to shift attention to another matter. Students sometimes cooperate in establishing new activities to counter the teacher's objectives for a class. Playing a game of Xs and

Os instead of listening to the teacher is one way of starting counteractivities in the classroom.

Alienated students may try to create alternative realities for themselves by taking drugs or by establishing for themselves new visual fields instead of focussing on the teacher and regular class activities. At present Freeze and Armstrong are engaged in a study which is designed to test the hypothesis that public secondary schools encourage more than acceptable levels of student alienation. They hope to compare the public schools with other learning environments, such as "free schools," which do not elicit the same degree of student alienation.

WHAT IS ALIENATED BEHAVIOR?

Alienated students have had difficulty relating their own experience to the experiences provided by the school. Because this situation has existed for many students throughout their formal schooling, some of these alienated students have become very cynical about the school's ability to meet their needs in the future. Disillusioned about his education, the alienated student often feels that, even if he did "play the game" at school, his chances of personally benefiting from compliance would still be very slim.

Robert K. Merton's classical studies on "anomie" help us to better understand what is meant by the term *alienation*. He describes the alienated person as one who is *"in* society but not *of* it."[1] The alienated student is one who is still in school, even though he is not *interested* in school. He may be in school simply because he has never thought of what he could do as an alternative.

Merton also points out that alienated individuals are many times resigned to failure regarding the attainment of personal goals. He stated that the alienated show an inability to adopt illegitimate means of obtaining their goals because of "internalized prohibitions." The reason for this, according to Merton, is that the "retreatist" (alienated) subculture has not fully renounced the dominant culture's success goals. The alien solves this dilemma by eliminating from his thought both the goals and the means of achieving them. Merton's "rebel," or the person we might be referring to as the "activist," also rejects the dominant culture's goals but usually substitutes new goals and new methods of obtaining the goals.

THE RESPONSIBILITY OF THE SCHOOL

Writing in *Weékend Magazine*, Gordon Green says that, to any educator with the courage to be honest about it, "it must be painfully clear that our modern super-duper high schools are a fantastic failure." Green states that the present educational system takes almost no account of a teacher's personality and his ability to communicate to students. Even if a teacher has the basic communication skills, it has become too difficult for the average teacher to know his pupils. Classes and students are computerized and little time is spent on any individual student's problems. Green quotes a guidance department head, Terry Callaghan, as saying, "Of all the elements missing in our large high schools today, the most critical is the personal relationship. . . . Human development requires interaction and involvement with others, and our large, comprehensive high schools provide little opportunity for that." Green concludes that we are now graduating the loneliest young people this country has ever seen.[2]

Other students are alienated for different reasons. Some students in "university bound" high school programs do not plan to attend university. Certain students claim they are not interested in certain subjects that they are required to take. On the other hand, many students who are in the "nonuniversity track," feel that they are in school merely to collect "a piece of paper" which will allow them to get a job. Other students say that they attend school only because there is nothing else to do. Certain students have felt so alienated that they have symbolically "waved good-bye" to the entire educational process. Someone has said that the alienated student has two choices: drop out and "turn on" (leave school and take dope), or "turn off" and stay in (learn to be selectively inattentive while remaining in school). What kind of school conditions would trigger these rejection responses?

Many of the social conditions that foster alienation range far beyond the classroom. However, there are signs which indicate that the school itself is largely to blame. Several school principals have suggested that one alienation-producing effect of the school concerns the fact that it may cause certain students to develop uncertainty concerning their own acceptability. The "I am a poor scholar" stigma is one kind of alienating effect of unsatisfactory relations between students and the school. A debased concept of oneself is considered to be one kind of self-estrangement.

In other cases, certain students are almost taught to be alienated. Underprivileged students may learn by experience that there are different rewards for equal efforts. In other words, they believe that the pay-off for their own effort is not commensurate with the pay-off given to other students for the same effort. A feeling of injustice and futility may result from this felt discrimination. A cult of alienation may emerge among the overprivileged as well. Some teachers give their students the impression that "university bound" students are superior. If certain students begin to believe that they are the cream of the crop, they form cliques which tend to become quite exclusive and snobbish. Snobbish disaffiliation can be viewed as one form of alienation.

INTERVIEWS WITH ALIENATED STUDENTS

In order to understand the reasons for alienation, we interviewed many high school students whom guidance counsellors identified as being alienated. The negative attitudes of most of these students were usually not supplemented by suggestions as to how the school could be improved. The student in the following interview showed signs of thinking of himself as an unacceptable person and felt that even his friends didn't understand him. It was doubtful if he had any close friends. The student did not belong to any school clubs. He attended no school functions or extracurricular activities. It was also difficult to get the student talking. Like so many of the alienated students interviewed, he seemed to be somewhat introverted and uncommunicative. He opened up somewhat on the topic of hallucinogenic drugs which he used "on occasion." His remarks concerning the idea that school forces a person to think in line with its own values constitute a recurrent theme among the alienated, who seem to think that school only reflects the values of a society with which they happen to disagree.

Interviewer: How do you like school?

Student: I hate it.

Interviewer: What is the problem?

Student: I don't know. Nothing happens here.

Interviewer: If you hate school you must be against something specific about the school.

Student: It forces you to think the way it wants you to think.

Interviewer: Anything else?

Student: Some teachers are on their own ego-trips. They force you to do things which they say are important, but which you know very well have nothing to do with your future.

Interviewer: What would you do to change the school if you had a chance?

Student: I wouldn't know where to start. Everything needs to be reorganized.

Interviewer: What things?

Student: It's hard to say. Get rid of teachers and get some new subjects.

Interviewer: Don't you need teachers?

Student: If they really tried to help you it might be okay. But most teachers don't try to understand where your "head is at." They just pump all this "you need this, you should do that, shit at you."

Interviewer: Do many other students feel the way you do?

Student: Some of them do—the ones who do any thinking.

Interviewer: How do you know they do any thinking?
Student: Well, anybody in his right mind has to be opposed to the way this school is run.
Interviewer: But do you think many students are opposed?
Student: Most of them don't think. The students in this school are a drag.
Interviewer: Do you have many close friends among other students?
Student: Not really. I make my friends outside of the school.
Interviewer: Whom do you associate with outside the school?
Student: Mostly "heads."
Interviewer: Who are they?
Student: They (heads) don't hassle you. They have their heads together.
Interviewer: Do you have anyone who is a particularly close friend?
Student: Not really.

SOCIOLOGICAL PERSPECTIVES ON STUDENT ALIENATION

Disaffiliation, disassociation, and *disengagement* are terms which are sometimes used to qualify the concept of alienation. However, these concepts are no less vague than the concept of alienation itself. Therefore, we will use the term "student alienation" and define it as an unsatisfactory relationship that is found to exist between a significant number of students and the schools they attend.

Alienation is revolutionary when one views it from a political perspective. According to Jean-Francois Revel, when a society declines seriously, it is sometimes because of an internal absenteeism, because its people have discovered new forms of commitment.[3] Those who adopt these new commitments are to be considered as part of the "counterculture." Students who become alienated constitute part of the counterculture in the school.

Eric Fromm has regarded alienation as a man's loss of sense of who he is in terms of his own particular powers and abilities.[4] An alienated person is not able to strongly identify with the larger social system of which he is a part, because he cannot exercise his own powers or express his own personality within the milieu generated by that system.

One common denominator of alienation is that the alienated person tends to retreat from situations which involve commitment. In some, but not all, cases this retreat indicates an attitude of scorn for society. In other cases, it merely signifies a wish not to become involved. Keniston conceives of alienated students as those who consciously repudiate and reject commonly accepted norms and values.[5] Alienation is explained by Keniston as an entire and radical reaction to a technological and depersonalized society. The alienated individual "turns off" or becomes insensitive to the usual demands and incentives given to him by main-stream culture. He may "turn on" to new stimuli that enable him to experience new sensations without going beyond himself. The search for ways to intensify present experience in a passive manner would help to account for the psychedelic revolution, including the use of mind-expanding drugs and the rebirth of mysticism.

Keniston thought of alienation as "unprogrammatic" because the alienated are iconoclasts lacking constructive ideas about the direction of change. They reject society but they do not offer new solutions. They distrust highly committed and overzealous people who show an interest in politics and institutions. The alienated, unlike the activists, tend to retreat into shells of isolation.

Melvin Seeman, a social psychologist at the University of Cali-fornia, Los Angeles, has developed a popular analytic instrument which attempts to measure some of the underlying dimensions of alienation. Each of Seeman's dimensions provides a focal point for discussion con-cerning conditions within the student's life which contribute to his feel-ing of alienation. Before describing some of the possible conditions which may be antecedent to each dimension of alienation, it is necessary to briefly define each of those dimensions.

- Seeman's first dimension of alienation is *powerlessness*. Powerless-ness was defined as "the expectancy of probability held by the indi-vidual that his own behavior cannot determine the occurrence of the outcomes or reinforcement he seeks."[6]

- *Meaninglessness* is a second dimension of alienation which Seeman describes as characterized by a "low expectancy that satisfactory predictions about future outcomes of behavior can be made."[7]

- The third referent of alienation relates to what Durkheim and Merton call *anomie*. Seeman calls this dimension *normlessness*, or cynicism. Normlessness occurs when social norms cease to influence behavior. Seeman defines normlessness as "a high expectancy held by the individual that socially unapproved behaviors are required to achieve given goals."[8]

- A fourth type of alienation is *social isolation*. There are many forms of social isolation, but one common characteristic of the isolated is that they "assign low reward value to goals or beliefs that are typically highly valued in the given society."[9] Isolation is caused by the fact that the individual has little desire to share commonly accepted rewards.

- Fifth, alienation may refer to *self-estrangement*. The person who is alienated from himself may have lost contact with his basic needs. The self-estranged person may feel that he has failed to realize his full human potential. He is that person whose day-to-day actions have ceased serving his/her real needs. He may govern his behavior to achieve anticipated future rewards that are probably more extrinsic than intrinsic.

● More recently, Seeman has spoken of *cultural estrangement*—the individual's removal from cultural values.[10] He uses, as an example of cultural estrangement, the artist or revolutionary who rejects the goals and values of his community. The culturally estranged person is sharply aware of the differences between the realities of his cultural milieu and his own vision of what culture could or should be.

POWERLESSNESS CREATED BY THE SCHOOL

Why should today's student feel powerless? Hasn't he been given his share of attention in the media? Hasn't he received his share of consumer goods and services? Doesn't he captivate adult attention with his constantly changing language and dress? Don't his parents and teachers spend enough time trying to figure out how to communicate with him?

Student powerlessness may be related to the tendency of teachers and administrators to undermine the integrity and motivation of students. For example, a young mother or a girl who assumes a good deal of responsibility around her home in her role as "mother" may come to school rather fatigued, or without completing her homework, only to confront some insensitive teacher who inquires, "What is the matter, didn't you understand the assignment?" Students may have a tendency to acquiesce in such situations without bothering to explain the problem. Explanation many times entails embarrassment because it involves admitting such things as the fact that the parents are unable to afford adequate babysitting. So, rather than fight back, the girl may accept the treatment which is usually given to irresponsible adolescents. The damage inflicted on the psyche due to unjustifiable harassments by insensitive teachers is sometimes hard to overcome.

Some students cannot compete under conditions dictated by the school. Many talented students have been urged to keep up academically, when more effort should be spent on their attempting to become good writers, artists, sportsmen, or scientists in their own right. Student culture, student music, student politics, and student expressions of other sorts are many times not regarded by teachers as the proper activities of the school. Some educators are of the firm opinion that students should be "educated" or "socialized" to conform to an adult society which possesses predetermined economic, social, and political qualities. Education then becomes the business of tailoring individuals to fit into a system with such qualities. These people believe that little effort should be expended on educating individuals who would be prepared to modify present social, political, and economic conditions. The results of all this are that students lack the feeling that their own needs are being considered by the school; intrinsic interests of the student are de-emphasized; and the seeds of powerlessness are sown in what becomes a self-fulfilling prophecy—powerlessness breeds powerlessness.

ON RENDERING SCHOOL LIFE MEANINGLESS

We have all witnessed many students who have told us that their courses, curriculum, examinations, and the instructional techniques of many teachers are irrelevant. Many students today feel that they cannot relate to the educational materials and processes to which they are being exposed. These students find little personal meaning in doing what the school requires them to do. It is not hard to understand how some of the trivia included in many course outlines and lesson plans contribute to the perception of irrelevance. When students are not able to see that the activity of the classroom is useful in assisting them in reaching their own personal goals, it is time for the educator to think seriously about what he is doing.

Another fact that has been impressed upon us from many directions is that disadvantaged children fail to relate to curricular materials, textbooks, and teachers that are only reflective of a middle class ethic. Dick and Jane, kids from middle class suburbia, have little in common with kids from completely different cultural environments. Instructors and materials originating in the middle class culture do not always relate to the specific motives, drives, and values of children from less privileged environments whose focal concerns are much different. Teachers, by and large, have made too little effort to understand the experience of the underprivileged student. Teachers isolated from the life experience of their students cannot possibly communicate with them during their lessons, and lack of communication is the veritable hallmark of alienated relationships. Many bright students who are capable of comprehending deficiencies in the school are now demanding that the schools begin to serve the real needs of the student. But the question of what is truly worth-while subject matter is not simple. Neither is the question concerning what kind of education best prepares the student to work and to cope with practical problems facing him daily.

Students must become bewildered when they try to understand the real motives or rationale of the authorities who administer the educational system. When the student begins to feel that what he/she is doing is quite trivial to the wider goals of society, a feeling of meaninglessness ensues. Sociologists have found that people who study or work simply to accomplish the internal goals of a bureaucratic system often become only objects to be regulated or trained in a very impersonal manner. Ronald Urick has pointed out that manager-bureaucrats juggle persons into categorized, rank-ordered positions.[11] These bureaucrats manipulate people in terms of quantity. It can be seen that, owing to the size of most modern schools, no organic, voluntary cooperation develops between the individuals and groups that make up the school's population. Bureaucratic procedure may be one of the fundamental reasons for lack of spontaneity in student-student as well as student-teacher relations.

NORMLESSNESS AND THE SCHOOL

Sociologists such as Durkheim have told us that people experience normlessness during periods when institutional norms and values are being questioned. When people are unsure about traditional norms and uncertain about accepting new norms and values, they are characterized by what Durkheim and Merton call "anomie." The student may become alienated from the school when he cannot identify with its norms or when the school has no specific and identifiable norms or values with which the student can identify.

A school dominated by principles of compromise and political expedience may be lacking in values which would be accepted by most students. It is the author's opinion that lack of values constitutes one of the major crises of the "liberal" school in the overly liberal society. This value vacuum has been created since the leaders of our educational institutions lack commitment to any combinations of norms which are perceived as valid by the student. Liberal educators pride themselves on moulding curriculum that is "value-free." Teachers, professing an unlimited confidence in science, sometimes discredit the importance of values and intuition in learning. Religion and moral values are disregarded by many secular educators. The public school in the Western world emphasizes the teaching of tolerance and compromise at the expense of avoiding intense minority opinion and both positive and negative expressions of iconoclasm and reconstruction.

Quite commonly, it is accepted that religious and moral values decline in importance from the freshman to the senior year. This decline may be related to the fact that students seem to lack a sense of direction and that they seem unable to replace values which may have been destroyed by the educational process itself. These students have been left hanging in a religious and ethical void. If we program our youth to a value-free mentality, we should not be astounded if some of them respond with a value-free political movement, such as nihilism. Nor, on the other hand, should we be surprised if some youth respond by entirely rejecting their education, and upon realizing their deprivation, advance an ethic which diametrically opposes their elders. Thus we see among youthful protesters some absolutists and moral extremists who have completely disaffiliated themselves from society. Today's students almost totally reject "liberal" trends in education because liberalism, in practice, has only pretended to be value-free. In any case, the values of the "liberal" are regarded by the alienated as the values of the status quo. Even the radicals reject liberal values which are formed by compromise and which do not permit any complete and thoroughgoing scrutiny and alteration of present institutions.

Another assumption held by liberal educators is that the best political solution is the one which serves all people equally. This argument is sometimes faulty. The premise that "all people should be treated equally" assumes that all people have similar needs. This may not be true. Furthermore, it is doubtful that many people can identify with organizations based solely on principles of compromise and public opinion. Public opinion, by definition, is at variance with individual opinion because it is developed through the modification of individual beliefs. By the time an opinion is stated in terms of a median, or an average, the individual man has usually become apathetic in terms of his adherence to or acceptance of it. In considering the question of minorities we might ask, "What room is there for the expression of strong minority positions in today's high school?" My teaching experience has led me to believe that minority opinion is often squelched, even in the most liberal of Canadian high schools.

ISOLATION IN THE SCHOOL

Feelings of isolation and loneliness are commonly found among students who attend large, bureaucratic, urban schools. We might understand the students' feeling of anonymity if we place ourselves in the position of the freshman who enters a large high school for the first time. The freshman notices that the school's halls are filled with seemingly endless rows of locker spaces. The lockers themselves may strike one as being very representative of the "little boxes" that most people occupy in technocratic bureaucracies. Many students have told me they have the feeling that no one in the school really cares about them. Their feeling of isolation is complicated by bewilderment at all the required "routine" procedures which are programmed into the daily life of the school.

Students also complain that adequate guidance counselling is missing from their experience. Often, they say, counsellors are "system people" and not really concerned about the students' personal, academic, and vocational problems. The counsellors, of course, are regulated by the necessity of advising too many students.

One of the most inhumane aspects of today's high school is that it does not provide time for students to socialize among themselves in a relaxed and casual manner; many schools literally push their students from class to class by providing the shortest possible class breaks. The rationale given by principals for this practice is that "students won't waste valuable study time," or that "short class breaks prevent students from wandering aimlessly in the halls." Overly abbreviated class breaks don't satisfy the student's need to relax, have an occasional "rap" with a friend, or discuss important events with people he doesn't otherwise see. Furthermore, too few schools have allocated sufficient space for voluntary student activities. Couple these bureaucratic difficulties with the personality problems many students experience and it all amounts to the fact that modern schools are becoming very impersonal.

CONTRIBUTION OF THE SCHOOL TO SELF-ESTRANGEMENT

Sometimes the school makes demands on the student which are totally inconsistent with his personal needs. When this happens the student must learn to separate school activities from other more interesting activities. In effect, the student has to develop two personalities and two respective sets of behaviors. One part of the student's personality must ritualistically accommodate to the expectations of the school. The other part represents his real interest, which is more intrinsically motivated. The part of the personality that is invested in the classroom responds only passively to the necessary activity demanded by the teacher. Due to the competition between the needs of the "actual self" and those exacted by the school, the student becomes somewhat schizophrenic. He separates school, which is dull and routine, from the rest of life, which is more spontaneous and satisfying in terms of his own interest. The important human needs of a student are many times overlooked by his educators. Required school activities are many times alien to self-confirmation and personal growth. Too little emphasis in school subjects has been placed upon finding out who one is, or what one's tradition has been, and what constitutes one's own identity. Certainly, too little importance has been given to the students' need to be different, deviant, or unique.

In order that students develop a sense of personal integration, we must teach them to follow their own divergent interests and discover their own talents. Many curriculum materials, especially mass-produced and technology-assisted materials, have had the effect of teaching all students the same thing. It is very difficult to motivate students when they are all expected to end up at the same place, and when personal choice is minimized in the learning experience. It is extremely difficult for a person to be an individual if he is required to be inculcated with the same information as everyone else. Educators have been talking about the need for individualized instruction, but individualization has been all too often operationalized to mean "how to become the same as everyone else at your own pace." Promoters of individually prescribed programs have still failed to realize that children have their own unique learning styles, that they learn in different ways, at different times, and at different rates. The emphasis on diversity and individuality has been missing in those schools whose primary orientation has been one of homogenization. Homogenization of human experience is almost always alienating for the individual.

CULTURAL ESTRANGEMENT

Public schools are seen by the student counterculture as giving disproportionate emphasis to the goals of a too-pragmatic society dominated by rationalistic, analytic, and linear thought. The perceptions of youth in the counterculture have been influenced by such things as the ecstatic radicalism of William Blake, the romanticism of T. S. Eliot, the ideas of Edgar Caycee on evolution of the spirit, and the mysticism of Eastern religion. Such thought is much less analytical than Western thought. Many students today are familiar with the teachings of Hare Krishna, Zen, and I Ching, Sufi, early Christianity, and many other religious and philosophical systems. Most public school teachers have not been exposed to these religions and philosophies. Certain students may be more concerned about karma and sartori than about planning their futures. This trend is very disconcerting to the more compulsive and career-oriented teachers and administrators.

The educational establishment has resisted the necessity of coming to terms with the idealism, mysticism, and romanticism of the younger generation. Therefore, the school has been rejected as irrelevant, counter-revolutionary, and oppressive. Marcuse's "Great Refusal" refers to the counterculture's decision to have little to do with a society that has refused almost entirely to acknowledge the experiential validity of the younger generation.

In an article called "Bob Dylan and the Poetry of Salvation," sociologist Steven Goldberg has attempted to interpret, in part, what it means to be a mystic.[12] Goldberg claims that the mystic has always been able to see what the scientist is only beginning to see—that all distinction is illusory.

In his mysticism, man attempts to uncover the meaning behind his own existence. Perhaps he finds that everything is meaningless. Other mystics feel that one or another kind of mystical experience allows each man to locate himself as a meaningful part of the universal flow. The mystic usually rejects the statisticians' concept of random distribution. He believes that every event is meaningful and significant if one chooses to acknowledge the meaning of that event.

How, then, can the experience of the mystic be reconciled with the experience of the scientist? The problem of reconciling the "straight" community and the counterculture is a problem of equal magnitude. Most educators today know very little about current themes in the student counterculture. Many teachers dismiss the writings of Ginsberg, Watts, and Leary as being bizarre. Such cultural deprivation leads to estrangement—student from society and society from student.

HABITUAL DRUG USE AS A FORM OF ALIENATION

Habitual nonmedical use of drugs is related to alienation. Drugs provide a "nonactivist" (alienated) method of altering one's experience. It is a nonactivist method because the drug user does not depend upon interaction with anyone else. His change of experience and perception happens as a result of a simple act like "popping a pill" or "doing up" with a needle. While "stoned" his experience is uniquely personal. Habitual drug use, therefore, represents autocentric or narcissistic behavior. Drug taking can be described as "alienated" rather than "social" behavior.

My theory regarding the huge increase of the nonmedical use of drugs in our society is linked to the Keniston speculation about the alienated youths' "search for sentience" which seems prevalent in postadolescent Americans and Canadians.[13] By "search for sentience" Keniston means the desire to achieve experience and stimulation while maintaining an essentially nonactive approach to one's environment. The pattern of acquiescent experiencing probably begins at a very early age in our society. Parents and teachers heap toys and artifacts galore upon their children and students. The child's world is made up of insensible, incomprehensible wonderment which requires no energetic movement or problem-solving activity on his part. He is continually presented and confronted with new objects of unusual shape and color. His nonactivity is later reinforced by electronic stimulation such as television and other media experiences, all of which provide instant entertainment for minimal effort.

By postadolescence these overstimulated children have vicariously lived through a wide variety of experiences. They are understandably unimpressed with less dramatic attempts to entertain them. Teachers and preachers bore them with their monotone voices and unidimensional presentations. These students begin to long for the blissful state of childhood which the unconscious recalls as a time of spectacular fascination and novelty. Lacking the energy to create a similarly stimulating environment as an adolescent, the understimulated student may learn one day that his earlier experiences can be simulated by taking a drug. A world of pleasant illusion is created in his head which does not depend upon much effort. "Popping a pill" or "taking a fix" can recreate the multi-dimensional world of stereophonic technicolor which is reminiscent of his youth. The fact that this world of illusion is chaotic and asocial does not really matter. The array of sights and sounds provided in the "stoned" experience are functional in alleviating his boredom with the real world.

One should never be tempted to lump drug users into the same category. Occasional marijuana and hashish users are very different, dispositionally and sociologically, from chemical users who take such drugs as LSD, speed, heroin, MDA, or other chemicals.

The Le Dain Commission reports that certain characteristics are associated with certain patterns of drug use.[14] Shortly, a case study concerning an amphetamine user will be presented. The Le Dain treatment report claims that amphetamine addicts ("speeders") are often found to lack self-esteem and often have alcoholic fathers. It would be difficult to correlate these two factors with incidence of hashish use. Certain personality variables are related to the habitual user's choice of drug. In the case of the amphetamine user, elevation of self-esteem seems to be a prerequisite for rehabilitation.

"Soft" drug users sometimes regard "speed freaks" as "jocks" in disguise. *Jock* is a slang term for someone who is thought to overemphasize power, physical prowess, and competition, especially in athletics. The soft drug user views the speeder as one who has an unusual need to impress other people. If this need to impress is so, it may result from a basic insecurity. Instead of competing in the area of athletics, the speeder turns to the competition of taking larger and larger dosages of speed. Quite commonly a speeder might tell a therapist that he "hit up" an unusual amount of speed. The therapist may know that the bragged-about dosage would probably kill any normal person. While stoned, amphetamine users experience personal confidence that may compensate for their usual lack of certainty. Some speeders have delusions of personal power, influence, and magnetism. These feelings are quite contrary to the feelings of the soft drug user. Hashish and marijuana have the reported effect of slowing the user down and relaxing him. Understandably, the predisposition to desire "speeding up" or "slowing down" is related to other personality as well as circumstantial variables.

The following case study concerns one amphetamine addict who used speed, both orally and by injection—"mainlining"—over a period of three and a half years. Amphetamine injections are often applied in "runs." A *run* is a series of injections done in a relatively short period of time. Runs may be done privately or collectively. When done collectively, a strange form of unselfishness among the users sometimes prevails. Speeders show their generosity by giving the drug to each other whether or not everyone can afford to pay for it. Supporting someone else's habit, although regarded as "sick" by straight society, helps to justify the speeder's actions because he contrasts his charity with the selfishness and materialism which he sees in the rest of society. These rather distorted values indicate the degree of alienation of the speed user from society-at-large.

ALIENATION AND ADDICTION—A CASE STUDY

Peter is a school drop-out who had been using drugs, especially speed, for over four years. He had been in and out of high school about twenty times. He provided a classic example of an extremely alienated youth who had withdrawn from society because he felt that he could not cope with its demands.

Peter was the second youngest of thirteen children living with their parents in a town of five thousand people in eastern Canada. He was first exposed to drugs at the age of fourteen. At sixteen he was trafficking drugs. At eighteen, with a ten-thousand-dollar down payment gleaned from his earnings as a trafficker, he bought a section of land in northern Ontario. Even though he had plans to farm the land, his property soon turned into a large arsenal for drug distribution in the Ottawa Valley. Over a period of a few months, twenty-two high school drop-outs joined Peter on the farm. It wasn't long before Peter had them all "turned on" to speed. Many of these young people, like Peter, had lived most of their lives moving from one part of Canada to another, and even to other parts of the world. Their transient backgrounds may be related to their problems.

One time Peter "over-amped" while using speed. "Over-amping" is the step immediately prior to "overdosing," which in the drug culture always means death. Fortunately, someone found Peter in a semiconscious state near his farm and took him to a hospital. During his stay in the hospital Peter procured as many illegal drugs from undisclosed sources as he did prior to his hospitalization. Peter also claims that the doctors allowed him to make his own prescriptions because they didn't know as well as he, how the drugs affected him.

After a couple of months in the hospital, Peter was referred to Madonna House, a Catholic commune (the people at Madonna say community rather than commune) in a rural environment. At Madonna he was aided in reconstructing his life. He gradually rebuilt his body through physical work and good food. Herbs were prepared which he used on a regular basis. The people of Madonna assisted Peter throughout the difficult stages of physical and psychological withdrawal.

After recuperating for three months Peter decided to leave Madonna House. He came and lived in Kingston for a short period of time before "hitting the road" in the summer months. During this time he

spoke to university classes about drugs and his own reasons for becoming involved in the drug scene. Peter told the university students that
his own background was a very unhappy one. He felt that his parents
had not really cared for him and there appeared to be a very inadequate
relationship between him and his father who was an alcoholic. Although
some of Peter's brothers and sisters had continued their educations even
beyond the high school level, Peter felt that he had very little chance of
following in his siblings' footsteps. He failed to see any future for himself in going to school. He said that his teachers hated and always
"picked on" him. He had been expelled from school as often as he had
left voluntarily. He was intelligent but seemed to lack confidence in himself and described himself as the black sheep of his family as well as of
his school.

When Peter came to Kingston he was only eighteen and still
owned his farm even though he was not living on it; he later lost the
farm because he was unable to keep up the payments. He did not want
to go back to his property as long as the drop-outs he had invited to
live with him remained there. Peter wanted to rehabilitate himself. He
had quit taking drugs. His main problem was that he still had to face
two trials on drug counts, which almost certainly meant at least one jail
sentence. He wanted to begin farming but he knew that the care of his
property, once he got rid of all the drop-outs, would be interrupted by
the jail sentence.

Peter started back to school in the fall of 1971 but his schooling
came to an abrupt halt when he found himself convicted and sent off
to jail. He had been "busted" a year earlier by a "nark" (informer) who
had taken Peter into his confidence. The informer had come to live on
Peter's farm. During his stay, according to Peter, the informer had even
"hit-up" on speed along with the rest of the people who lived on the
farm. Peter was charged with dealing dope to the informer. Consequently he found himself in jail.

While serving his sentence, Peter became embittered and reverted
to his former attitudes and habits. When he left jail he once again
turned to speed. Being somewhat ashamed of himself and his condition,
he did not go directly to the people who may have been able to help
him. Rather, he went to live in a house in Toronto where several of his
old acquaintances lived. He found his friends still very involved in the
drug scene. It was not long before he started trafficking drugs again.
One time he was "ripped off" for a fairly sizable quantity of speed which
had been supplied to him by the "Mafia." One cannot market drugs
which he does not have, but Peter was considered to owe the "Mafia"
suppliers several hundred dollars for the lost drugs. When he could not
pay, the suppliers threatened his life. Peter knew about other cases of
assault and even murder when traffickers were unable to pay their debts

or when they transgressed upon the other drug dealers' marketing areas.

It was at this point that Peter telephoned and asked for protection and help. Someone went to Toronto to get him and took him to a safe place for a few days. During this time Peter tried to "dry out" and "work down" off the heavy chemicals he had been into. He obtained some Valium and smoked a little grass. After some horrible nightmares and a painful withdrawal period, he started to feel a little better.

When the worst period of withdrawal was over Peter started to travel again. Later he returned to a correctional training centre where he had been sent after being convicted in his second trial. The training centre, unlike the jail, seemed to have a positive effect upon Peter. He rested and began doing some fairly meaningful work. He claimed to be getting healthier and happier and generally seemed to be "getting his head back together." He wanted to get a job at the end of his term in the training centre.

Peter, at this time, was still in a fairly difficult position. He wanted to finish high school but he was not sure how the teachers and other students would respond to him. His coordination was not particularly good. The last time he had been in school his physical education teacher had made totally unrealistic demands of him. Peter's ability to concentrate had also diminished, and at the slightest suggestion some of his old "rushes" would return. He occasionally had a sharp pain in his liver, which he hoped was not damaged to the point of endangering his life.

A CHALLENGE FOR EDUCATORS

Problems such as Peter experienced are very real to long-term heavy speed users. Educators must learn to cope with the unique problems faced by Peter and the many students in similar situations. If anything is to be done to educate alienated drug addicts, much patience and understanding will be required from the educators who deal with them.

In addressing themselves to the complex drug problem, educators must make a stronger effort to understand the drug abuser and must try to effect student and adult attitudinal and behavioral change. This implies the need for broad-scale teacher training and retraining in new approaches to the problem. The National Clearinghouse for Drug Abuse Information in Washington, D.C., recommends that educators develop a long-range program to prepare health educators and other school personnel who need to concentrate on the problem of drug abuse. There must also be cooperation involving other segments of the community in a joint effort with the school if the mounting trend of drug abuse is to be reversed.

A STUDY ON DRUGS AND THE DROP-OUT

Motivated by an interest in students and ex-students with problems such as Peter's, we set out in the summers of 1971 and 1972 to study school drop-outs and transient youths involved with drugs. We interviewed 260 youths from fourteen to twenty years of age who visited overnight youth hostels in eastern Canada. We found that school drop-outs constituted close to half the transient population. Only about one-third of the drop-outs among the transients had been expelled or had become discouraged because of scholastic failure. Two-thirds had left school voluntarily, usually for the reason that they had grown tired of the monotony of school and wanted to try something else and have new experiences.

The transient sample was also found to include large numbers of drug users. The findings indicated very clearly that drug use was related to time lost from school as well as to dropping out of school. It is interesting that about half the drug users who dropped out of school left during the tenth grade. The reasons for the disproportionate number of students who leave school at this particular time should probably be investigated. One reason could be that most students become sixteen years of age during tenth grade, and they reach the age when they can legally leave school. Perhaps some students would complete high school if they could be persuaded to remain throughout the tenth grade.

Loss of time from school by students actually in attendance was also highest in grade ten. Student absences during grade ten were significantly and positively correlated with their corresponding use of at least sixteen separate drugs which were investigated. At other grade levels the use of only four to six drugs was found to be related to nonattendance. These results show that grade ten is a crucial year in considering the drug and drop-out problems.

The relationship between the extent of involvement with drugs and the student's absence from school can be looked at in another way by contrasting the total loss of time from school of the drug users as opposed to the nonusers (see figure). It was found that occasional soft drug users lost an average of 6.7 weeks of school for every three years in high school, whereas the non-users lost an average of only 4.7 weeks. Occasional soft and hard drug users lost 10.7 weeks per three years. Regular soft drug users lost 15.7 weeks, and regular hard and soft drug users lost 16.3 weeks. It can be seen from these statistics that an escalation in total time lost was related to increasing involvement with drugs.

Some rough statistics can be given on the prevalence of drug use in the transient sample. Approximately 10 percent of the sample were using such narcotics as opium, morphine, heroin, codeine, and metha-

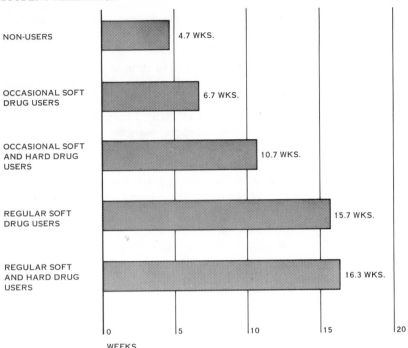

WEEKS

Drug Use and Loss of Time from School (during a 3-year period)

done at the time we interviewed them. Another 10 percent of the sample had tried these drugs but were not presently using them. Heroin is now the most popular narcotic.

The hallucinogens were quite another matter. Eighty to ninety percent of the transient sample were using marijuana and hashish at the time of the investigation. Over fifty percent of the sample had used, or were using, other hallucinogens such as mescaline, LSD, DMT, or STP.

Stimulants such as cocaine and speed (Benzedrine, Dexedrine, and Methedrine) were used by about 20 percent of the transient sample, Methedrine being the most popular drug among the "speeders." Only 5 to 10 percent of the sample used barbiturates (Nembutal, Deconal, phenobarbital, or Amytal) and other sedatives such as Equinal, Doriden, and Librium. Of these "downers," Deconal (also called Seconal) was most frequently used. About 5 percent of the sample had tried glue or solvents in the course of their drug use histories.

All the drop-outs in the sample were questioned about their reasons for leaving school. These reasons were categorized as forced decisions, such as expulsion, low achievement, illness, and financial necessity; and voluntary decisions, such as general dissatisfaction with school or a desire to try something new. Expulsion, however, was the nonattendance factor most related to drug use. Among the forty youths who had been forced to leave school, only four were non-users, and at least half were regular soft and hard drug users.

Educators sometimes assume that many drop-outs wish to return to school. Guidance counsellors often plan how to keep a student in school without giving much regard to the fact that the student himself does not want to stay. All the drop-outs in the study were asked to estimate their feelings of regret at having their formal educations interrupted. Those who had voluntarily dropped out showed very little regret regarding their decision to leave. Lack of regret was especially characteristic of drop-outs from higher income families, but it was true of many other drop-outs as well. For instance, the soft drug users seldom indicated any regret about losing time from school. It might be well for teachers, parents, and guidance counsellors to keep this lack of regret in mind when offering advice to the drop-out.

The regular hard drug users, on the whole, showed much more regret than did the non-users. Regret because of lost time was significantly and positively related to the frequency of use of at least a dozen hard drugs. Regret was especially related to the use of heroin ("smack"). Heroin was also the drug most associated with total time loss from school.

The transient drop-outs were asked if they felt the time they had lost from school was recoverable. Feelings of regret and optimism concerning recovery were significantly related. This optimism is not to be confused with actual likelihood of recovery. However, it would be interesting to do a follow-up study to test the relationship between optimism and actual recovery.

A most interesting finding is that many of the results indicated definite sex-related differences. The female transients lost more time from school than did their male peers. A consistent relationship existed between total time lost in each grade and being female. Although a moderate relationship existed between being female and restricting drug use to soft drugs, and the length of time using soft drugs prior to using hard drugs, being female was also related to the frequency of using "speeders" and certain "downers" such as Librium.

SUMMARY

One feature of the contemporary student mood is that many students feel alienated—not only from their schools and teachers, but also from themselves and society-at-large. Large, bureaucratic schools are probably partly to blame for student alienation. System constraints make it difficult to solve the problem of depersonalization in the schools. Since drug abuse is an important symptom of student depersonalization, the drug problem has been discussed as an outgrowth of extreme alienation, a condition that characterizes increasing numbers of high school students.

NOTES

1. Robert K. Merton, "Social Structure and Anomie," *American Sociological Review*, October 1938, pp. 672–82.
2. H. Gordon Green, "How Obsolete Are Our High Schools?" *Weekend Magazine*, March 11, 1972, pp. 8–11. Reprinted by special permission of Dr. H. Gordon Green, Ormstown, Quebec.
3. Jean-Francois Revel, *Without Marx or Jesus: The New American Revolution Has Begun*, trans. Jack Bernard (New York: Doubleday & Co., 1971).
4. Eric Fromm, *The Sane Society* (New York: Fawcett World Library, 1955).
5. Kenneth Keniston, *The Uncommitted: Alienated Youth in American Society* (New York: Harcourt, Brace & World, 1965).
6. Melvin Seeman, "On the Meaning of Alienation," *American Sociological Review*, December 1959, p. 784.
7. *Ibid.*, p. 786.
8. *Ibid.*, p. 788.
9. *Ibid.*, p. 789.
10. Melvin Seeman, "Alienation: A Map," *Psychology Today 5*, no. 3 (August 1971), pp. 82–84, 94–95.
11. Ronald Urick, *Alienation: Individual or Social Problem* (Englewood Cliffs, N.J.: Prentice-Hall, 1970), p. 62.
12. Steven Goldberg, "Bob Dylan and the Poetry of Salvation," *Saturday Review*, May 1970, pp. 43–46, 47.
13. Keniston, *The Uncommitted*, p. 181.
14. Gerald Le Dain (Chairman) Royal Commission of Inquiry into the Non-Medical Use of Drugs, *Treatment* (Ottawa: Information Canada, 1972), p. 33.

BIBLIOGRAPHY

Barakat, Habim Isber. "Alienation from the School System." Master's thesis, University of Michigan, 1966.

Blackburn, Donald J., and Patricia J. Storey. "The Dilemma of Migrating Rural Youth." School of Agricultural Economics and Extension Education, Ontario Agricultural College, 1972.

Blum, Richard H. *Students and Drugs and High School Observations*. San Francisco: Jossey-Bass, 1969.

Burton, Anthony. *The Horn and the Beanstalk: Problems and Possibilities in Canadian Education*. Montreal: Holt, Rinehart & Winston, 1972.

Gormley, Sheila. *Drugs and the Canadian Scene*. Toronto: Pagurian Press (distributed by Burns & MacEachern), 1970.

Hart, Leslie A. *The Classroom Disaster*. New York: Teachers College Press, 1969.

Hickerson, Nathaniel. *Education for Alienation*. Toronto: Prentice-Hall, 1966.

Holt, John. *How Children Fail*. New York: Dell Publishing Co., 1964.

———. *How Children Learn*. New York: Dell Publishing Co., 1967.

Horney, Karen. *Self Analysis*. New York: Norton & Co., 1942.

Jones, Richard Mathew. *Fantasy and Feeling in Education*. New York: New York University Press, 1968.

Josephson, Eric and Mary, eds. *Man Alone: Alienation in Modern Society*. New York: Dell Publishing Co., 1962.

Laing, Ronald D. *The Divided Self*. England: Tavistock, 1960.

Leonard, George Burr. *Education and Ecstasy*. New York: Dell Publishing Co., 1968.

Loken, Joel. Some Correlates of Alienation. Master's thesis, University of Calgary, 1968.

Love, Harold D. *Youth and the Drug Problem*. Springfield, Ill.: Thomas, 1971.

Marin, Peter and Albert Cohen. *Understanding Drug Abuse*. New York: Harper & Row, 1971.

Schacht, Richard. *Alienation*. Garden City, N.Y.: Doubleday & Co., 1970.

Siberman, Charles E. *Crisis in the Classroom*. New York: Random House, 1971.

Weinberg, Carl. "The School, the Society, and the Individual." In *Humanistic Foundations of Education*. Englewood Cliffs, N.J.: Prentice-Hall, 1972.

3 Student dissent

*Student dissent—"vociferous, active, resisting protest"—is
another dimension of student disaffection. Student alienation, if
it is a "chosen" posture, can be considered a type of revolt.
By actively opposing many of the programs and policies of the
institutions they participate in, student dissenters represent a
more overt type of protest. Radical dissenters cannot be
conceived simply as reformers, because reformers, strictly
speaking, are those who believe in adhering to constitutional
means of bringing about change. Because some use unlawful
tactics, student dissenters have been conceived as delinquents
rather than as reformers by teachers and school officials. This
delinquent stereotype does not always hold, for many (not all)
dissenters are constructive in their aims; their energetic criticism
and resistance sometimes force the educational authorities to
take action. In fact, students, and especially dissident
students, have discovered that by directly opposing their
educators they can often force changes in traditionally
unquestioned policies.*

STUDENTS TODAY not only actively challenge existing policies. They feel
they have a right to receive a high quality educational experience from
their teachers and their schools. They do not stand for mistreatment or
incompetence the way they once might have in a more authoritarian
system. When the right to receive a good education is threatened, some
students can be expected to take action. In the fall of 1972, Ontario
witnessed a rash of student strikes, ostensibly aimed at teachers who
were on their own Federation-sponsored "work-to-rule" strikes. Actually,
the student protests probably bolstered the teacher protests in putting
even more pressure on the school boards to improve teaching conditions in the schools. Even though the students appeared to be striking
against their teachers, it was the school board that stood to lose.

Student strikes, sit-ins, walkouts, and demonstrations are part of what is being termed "student dissent" in this book. Dissenting students, unlike the alienated, aggressively attack society while trying to implement change. The alienated have been described by Keniston as youth who draw into shells of social isolation; whereas the activists are usually willing to work hard in promoting change.[1]

CHANGES IN STUDENT DISSENT

It should be remembered that the angriest part of the student rebellion had terminated by 1972. Dick Kleiner, in an article appearing in the *Kingston Whig Standard*, refers to Irwin R. Blacker, who believes that the main reason for the change in student violence was economic, a by-product of depression. Kleiner quotes Chandler Harris as stating, "When the wolf is at the door, you want to chase him away and not raise hell."[2] Many students today have to work to make ends meet. So they either take fewer courses or they take more. In either case, they have not got time for such extracurricular activities as demonstrations.

Some students felt that militant activism did not accomplish very much in terms of bettering school conditions for themselves. During the past two years, high school administrations seem to be taking tougher stands against the student rebel. Blacker comments that there were days when school administrators shivered and cowered before the activists. "Now they are prepared to kick a student out like a shot."

Blacker, however, believes that the student rebellion was somewhat successful. Students had been given a somewhat stronger voice in school affairs. Before the rebellion, most students were not as able to talk to their teachers individually. Blacker feels that most teachers now attempt to form friendly, ongoing relationships with their students and make themselves available for individual consultation. A group of Ontario principals agreed in the spring of 1972 that pressure was being mounted by students on teachers who failed to communicate with their classes. These principals thought that student activism in the future could be directed more against the incompetent teacher than against the educational establishment.

Students still appear to be concerned about issues such as the ecological crisis. However, instead of marching, today's students may contribute to some organization which will lobby through its lawyers and political contacts to clean up the environment. Even though the general mood of students has changed, there are responsible activists in groups such as those concerned with the quality of the environment. The student activist of today is the student who is still alive to social and political problems. But instead of rioting, he might spend his time reading about the problems and discussing solutions with anyone who is interested. Much of his time might be spent in organizations designed to fight the problems through political techniques. However, these students are still "countercultural" in that they are working against the technological, materialistic, and consumption goals of the majority of people in the dominant society.

Definitions of contemporary student activism should include a reference to activists' life styles (action) as well as to their rhetoric. The life style of an activist is *confrontational*. Confrontation consists of bringing a social issue to a level of consciousness where it can be discussed and publicized. Confrontation usually involves the disruption of usual procedure and formal institutions. Confrontation involves a showdown between antagonistic forces where one of those forces is interested in inciting some social change.

The activist claims that he has the right to bring social concerns and problems to the surface because, only by facing up to these problems, will society be able to solve them. The activist feels that certain injustices and unreasonable practices have been kept far too long at a level where they cannot be readily observed and analysed. Some activists deliberately use "shock techniques" in order to make people think about problems. Additionally, the activist usually thinks of himself as a champion of the oppressed. Therefore, he may attempt to inform the underprivileged about the nature of their oppression.

The activist's belief in equality leads him to advocate "participatory democracy" as a mandatory quality of society. This idea implies that people should participate in all economic and political decisions that deeply affect their lives. Participatory democracy depends upon changes from centralized to more decentralized decision-making procedures in prevailing political processes. Activists claim that, without effective participation, a man is left in the ambiguous position of "experiencing himself as a powerless being," cut off from the meaning of his existence and alienated from himself as well as society.[3]

Activists compose only a small percentage of the student population in any school. Activists will not, for example, number more than forty in a typical city school of fifteen hundred students. Of this small number, only a few are willing to sacrifice the time and energy necessary to bring about the reforms they urge. Despite the minimal size of the activist core, large numbers of students lend their support to the radicals. There is no doubt that most students are disenchanted, uneasy, and even anxious about their place in the schools. The most obvious symptoms of this anxiety are lack of hope and confusion about the goals and purpose of life.

Adults are in danger of misunderstanding what it is that radical students are thinking and doing; they tend to fall back on the rather irrelevant comment that protest and dissent are part and parcel of student life in every generation. But today's unrest is not concerned with merely rearranging society or redistributing wealth. It is, instead, a truly radical criticism of society and a questioning of the meaning and purpose of life itself.

To understand the activists' approach to change, we must realize that for the activist, action and thought are only true when they are united. For this reason, we cannot successfully look for a collection of student revolutionary thought, for thought *is* revolution and revolution *is* thought. Because of this, student activism defies description or categorization under the normal classifications of behavior. Some attempts to do so have pushed the movement forward into the area of "happenings" which lie beyond the scope of formal logic.

THE UNDERGROUND PRESS

The student activist movement is now so diffuse and amorphous that it is difficult to make specific generalizations concerning its character. One only needs to read a few of the many Canadian underground newspapers in order to determine the wide variety of interests and activities within the activist movement. The following assortment of items appeared in one issue of a particularly good paper: an article on "hassles" between people who wanted to live in marginal dwellings on the outskirts of society, and municipalities who wanted to demolish their houses; a letter to the editor on "pluralism," by Philip Slater and Robert Theobald; a diary on the growth and fall of an experimental wilderness community; a historical sketch of the tradition of "intentional communities" and commune living; a section of information on organic gardening including various methods of composting, principles of nutrition, and information about cereal grains; a list of accommodations for those who wish to "crash" across Canada; and many interesting ads including the address of the author of *The Cultivator's Handbook of Marijuana.*

In spite of the tendency towards rhetoric, many underground papers, such as *Alternate Society* (Welland, Ontario), *The Source* (Ottawa), and *The Georgia Straight* (Vancouver), provide some very relevant reading. A minimum requirement of any well-informed teacher should be to read the various underground papers published in his area. In this way the teacher can keep informed on the patterns of behavior within the counterculture and among youth in general.

Another method of getting information is to read recently published paperbacks about the youth subculture. The *Strawberry Statement* (J. S. Kunen), *Our Time Is Now* (Kurt Vonnegut, Jr.), *Student Power and the Canadian Campus* (Tim and Julyan Reid), *High School Revo-*

lutionaries (Libarle and Seglison), *Student Protest* (McGuigan), and *The New Left in Canada* (Roussopoulos), which have been useful to some, are probably now outdated.[4] Educators who want to keep abreast of the activist scene will have to read new books.

Our Time Is Now is comprised of notes from the high school underground. It reports on radical activities particularly designed to affect the school and education. It summarizes many high school incidents involving confrontation of various sorts. Another book which takes a look at confrontation in the schools is *Conflict and Dissent in the High School* by Kenneth Fish.[5]

BEHAVIOR OF THE ACTIVISTS

Gary Rush, associate professor at Simon Fraser University, feels that student protest at the high school level tends to be apolitical and oriented to specific social issues (for example, dress norms, smoking, school rules). He has commented that student protest in the high school system seldom addresses central issues regarding the quality of education. Rush suspects that the indoctrination process in the public school system is sufficiently effective to prevent students from developing a class consciousness. Probably this prevents students from establishing the group feeling which is essential for effective dissent.

Fish on the other hand has written that he feels students are alive to the important issues.

Most students cherish humanistic values, in sharp contrast to the regimentation and institution-centered practices in schools. Listening to them, one has the feeling that the more verbal spokesmen have just returned from a workshop in sensitivity training, and that they are passionately seeking the fulfillment of a dream in which teachers have shaken off their customary institutional robot role. Speaking of teachers, a student says: "I want to communicate with him as a *person*; I want to break down that student-teacher role hang-up. . . . they're all hung up on their role; they're afraid to communicate with us *as people*; they're afraid that something about their authority or respect is going to be lost. We're looking for understanding; this is what is missing. There's a need for students and faculty to be *open* with each other."[6]

The rejection of grades and rewards and prizes has become one of the fundamental tactics of protest. Principals have disclosed the fact that, instead of praising the system, more and more valedictorians have been using their opportunity to address parents and teachers to strike out angrily against the educational system. Many prize-winning students have thrown away their medals, denounced the competitions as fraudulent and the pay-off as worthless. Charles Hampden-Turner claims, "We have a new intellectual class whose property is their education and their conscience, rather than money or land." He goes on to say:

> Since virtually all the psycho-social data indicate that these young radicals are remarkably gifted, developed and creative, it behooves us to examine the style and tactics of their revolt. What may appear to us initially as shocking deviation from the norms of polite society may in reality be a new consciousness, which in time we shall come to share.[7]

Student radicals in the high school have been actively organizing in recent years. Ombudsmen have been appointed in some centres to adjudicate on matters of educational grievance initiated by students. For instance, student radicals in Ottawa succeeded in gaining control of the Central Students' Council in 1970–71. In Toronto's North York, Ottawa, and several other centres, high school students have been constructing bills of rights which constitute written and legal statements of student civil liberties in the areas of free expression, privacy, and due process of law. Below are paraphrased the articles from one such bill of rights:

- Every student has the right to an educational environment best suited to his needs, interests, and abilities; and within the school environment the student, in consultation with his teacher(s), shall be able to determine the mode and direction his education shall take;
- Every student has the rights of freedom of speech, freedom of assembly, and freedom of the press, all subject to the standards of Canadian laws applicable to the general public;
- No student shall be subjected to any form of corporal punishment;
- No student is to be subjected to any form of intrusion of privacy of his person or belongings, and shall have access to all formal records which are kept concerning him;
- Students shall be guaranteed the opportunity of effective participation in the government of their school;
- Every student has the right to determine the method of his formal evaluation with his teacher(s); and,
- No group or person has any right to engage in any activity or perform any act aimed at the destruction of any of the rights and freedoms of others.

The League for Student Democracy (LSD) was established in 1970 and operated out of Toronto. The LSD had its origins in a North York high school in September 1969. A group of dissatisfied students met in secret and came to agreement—that the present education system was crassly materialistic, psychologically poisoning, and inherently undemocratic; that just teaching about the problems would solve nothing; that students are one of the most disorganized forces in our society; and that isolated protest in only one school would not remould the entire monolithic structure.

The league recruited high school leaders and interested students from over forty school locations across Ontario. The LSD was responsible for establishing the *Third Eye*, a student paper, which has helped in the task of expansion, petitioning, and organization. With a constitution formulated and policy determined, the league went on to its first technical campaign. It attained the right from the North York Board of Education for any student to address the board on any issue which affected them. The league encouraged a sit-in regarding the "slacks" issue in Hamilton, and found itself a force to be contended with. The LSD continued to do battle with the educational system in Ontario. It then engaged in a project designed to limit the power of the principal in the school system. This activity took the shape of a provincewide petition, a detailed brief, and a demonstration-presentation to the minister of education at Queen's Park.

Sometimes radical activity in the schools has been assisted by teachers who have given the students information which has assisted them in liberating themselves. For example, students in one Alberta school discovered that when teachers gave them detentions which kept them in the school beyond the regularly prescribed time of operation, those teachers were violating their legal rights. These Alberta students questioned the authority of the school to detain them beyond the time designated by law. Such examples indicate that students are beginning to recognize that they have power—power to organize, to influence, and to change the policies of their schools.

MORAL AND CREATIVE DEVELOPMENT OF THE DISSENTERS

In trying to understand the socialization process that has led a student to become a dissenter, it is insufficient to study the effects of various sociological forces that continually exert pressure. Socialization also involves the subject who is not just a passive victim of forces impinging upon him. Man is capable of responding selectively to various forces that seek to influence him. When socializing influences impinge on the individual, their actual effect is modified by the subject. Thus it is important to study the relevant aspects of the personality, values, and related internal forces, as well as to examine the external forces which operate upon the individual. Although major attention should be given to social background factors of the student dissenter, some attention should also be given to psychological factors.

McGuigan has suggested that because of the possibility of human extinction, there has arisen a greater need for universal communication. Under the threat of extinction a new generation has been born. McGuigan proposes that this new generation is unconsciously and implicitly different from all previous generations and it is the radical student who most ostensibly demonstrates the new mentality. For this reason the older generation finds it difficult to communicate with a genuinely radical student. According to McGuigan the two groups are so different logically, culturally, and semantically that communication becomes almost impossible.[8]

McGuigan does not feel that any set of traceable moral principles accounts for the gap in communication. However, in an article "Morals: Left and Right," Charles Hampden-Turner and Phillip Whitten attempt to show, through psychological research, that personal polarization between those of opposing ideological persuasions can be traced to differentiation in moral development.[9] Using Kolberg's model of moral development, they conclude that the counterculture has been necessitated in order to transcend cultural values characteristic of traditional, conservative, rule-centred teachers and parents. Hampden-Turner and Whitten have insinuated that activists in the counterculture show superior moral development and awareness. Charles Reich in his book, *The Greening of America*, alludes to the possibility of a new consciousness among today's youth. Most responsible activists are commonly regarded by sociologists as individuals characterized by Consciousness III which is Reich's most advanced stage of psycho-social development.

The foundation of Consciousness III is liberation. It comes into being the moment the individual frees himself from automatic acceptance of the imperatives of society and the false consciousness which society imposes. For example, the individual no longer accepts unthinkingly the personal goals proposed by society. Change of personal goals is one of the first and most basic elements of Consciousness III. The meaning of liberation is that the individual is free to build his own philosophy and values, his own life style and his own culture from a new beginning.

Consciousness III starts with self. . . . To start from self does not mean to be selfish. It means to start from premises based on human life and the rest of nature, rather than premises that are artificial products of the corporate state, such as power or status. It is not an "ego trip" but a radical subjectivity designed to find genuine values in a world whose official values are false and distorted. It is not egocentricity but honesty, wholeness, genuineness in all things. It starts from self because human life is found as individual units, not as corporations and institutions; its intent is to start from life. . . . Consciousness III postulates the absolute worth of every human being—every self. Consciousness III does not believe in the antagonistic or competitive doctrine of life. . . . Consciousness III rejects the whole concept of excellence and comparative merit. . . .

. . . The initial premise of self [in Consciouness III] leads not only to a critique of society, it also leads, in many representatives of Consciousness III, to a deep personal commitment to the welfare of the community. . . . the key to Consciousness III commitment lies in the concept of full personal responsibility. . . . One quality unites all aspects of the Consciousness III way of life: energy. It is the energy of enthusiasm, of happiness, of hope.[10]

Sociological theories alone have been unable to account for the variance between "political activists" and "nonactivists." That is why it is fruitful to examine the psychological variables which may contribute to the variance. Social psychologists have investigated some of the cognitive and affective correlates of activism. Merelman is one of the few who have stated that cognitive variation between individuals is important in determining political radicalism because only through the adoption of certain cognitive skills is one able to make the necessary linkages between ideas and events that facilitate an interest in political affairs.[11]

A comparison of creativity and habit may provide some theoretical perspective on the differences between those who advocate change and those who resist it. Creative man maximizes his ability to select and modify the forces which seek to influence and shape his behavior. Creativity is sometimes defined as the ability to comprehend alternative ways of behaving. (See Table 3.)

Table 3. Creative Man versus Man of Habit

Man of Habit	Creative Man
Dominated by processes of conditioning	More autonomous
Given to ritual	Maximizes on ability to select and . . .
Tends toward "embeddedness" and safety	Modify forces which seek to influence him
More conservative and dogmatic	Comprehends alternative ways of behaving
Emphasizes rote memory and command styles of teaching	More exploring and risk-taking
Not versatile in his behavior	Deviant and innovative
Cannot understand the creative person	Flexible

Retreat to safety becomes a familiar path of action for habitual man. However, some once-functional safety routes may become failure routes as a result of changing social conditions. It is at this point that alteration rather than persistence in traditional behavior is required.

Pure habit does not involve very much thought. Habit is based upon the fact that past behavior is still functional. Archconservatives may be creatures of habit. Psychologists have told us that a relationship exists between intelligence and radicalism and that certain so-called "deviant" members of society are frequently very ingenious innovators.

A creative, intelligent person is able to more fully comprehend the consequences of his actions in ways not immediately apparent to those dominated by habit. A habit may be so strong as to constitute a virtual block against learning a new response. People so dominated are termed "dogmatic." It has been demonstrated by Flacks, Keniston, and others that activists are not dogmatic. Rather they demonstrate a great deal of cognitive flexibility.[12]

Cognitive flexibility is not the only means of measuring the ability to respond in novel ways. Furthermore, certain things which reach the level of cognition do not necessarily filter down to the level of measurable, overt behavior. A new concept is required to differentiate people who are truly open to alternative behavior from those who can merely think about change. For instance, one may be able to espouse several styles of teaching along a continuum from the "command" style to the more pupil-directed "discovery" method. The advocates of the discovery method may not actually be able to teach by that method.

A term which could be utilized to refer to truly innovative persons is "person-openness." The individual characterized by such "openness" would be capable of allowing alternative ways of thinking to filter into his actual manner of life. The life style of such an individual would be regarded as radical to mainstream culture. However, that life style could be functional for the activist as well as prophetic for society. The truly open person is capable of living in a variety of ways, depending on circumstances. The open person is behaviorally versatile. However, some people who measure "flexible" on behavioral indices of cognitive flexibility, such as *Rokeach's Dogmatism Scale*, may be quite rigid in their actual behavior.

I once saw a student activist criticize a teacher for being so conservative and dogmatic. The teacher defended himself by stating that he had once filled out a questionnaire aimed at measuring liberal traits and that, out of a group of twenty subjects, he scored most liberal. This individual may serve as an example of a person who is *cognitively* open, but *behaviorally* closed.

In my own research I have tested the hypothesis concerning the creativity of student activists.[13] The results indicate a significant positive relationship between activism and creativity, which was validated objectively and clinically through the assistance of a neutral psychometrician. It is necessary for educators to understand some of the important psychological tendencies of student activists if they wish to cope with them and appreciate them for what they are.

DEMANDS OF DISSENTING STUDENTS AND TEACHERS

Perhaps it is time to consider seriously the charges levelled against the educational system by the more radical students. Frequently regarded as "system disturbers," the activists are seriously concerned about the failings of the educational system and its philosophy (or lack of it).

One demand of the radicals is for a change in the emphasis of many schools from that of pretending to prepare potential workers for particular jobs in the future to providing a more creative experience for each student in the present. Education, they say, has become a tool for an economic way of life that disregards certain aspects of human potential. The task of teaching has traditionally been to implement the master plan of some super system as provided in an "official" curriculum.

Some students today believe that education should provide an opportunity for the person being educated to pursue his own social and academic needs, rather than forcing the student to accept the educational goals of society and the school. Many activists feel that academic freedom is available only in the best schools. But the best schools are reserved for very few people. There is legitimate claim to the argument that if the educational system now exists only to discriminate against learners rather than to serve in a somewhat egalitarian fashion, it should be changed.

Students today tend to reject the idea of education occurring in a value-free vacuum. Nor do they feel that the present "progressive" or "liberal" model of education is really "value-free." Most of the activists interviewed regarded the present Canadian educational system as patterned on a model only pretending to be value-free, but which actually advances the values of the prevailing economic system. Like the alienated, activist leaders regard the value-free, or the pretended value-free, model of instruction as one of the prime reasons for the sterility of the present system. Certain educators have been operating on the basis of the "best for the most" philosophy of education for the past few decades. Obvious difficulties are created by the "best for the most" application of social policy. Some individuals and minority groups are overlooked. Students today generally desire a school that is swept clean of "prescriptive" curriculum theories and collective remediation. They want a society that is collective in the sense of people being interested in one another—not collective in terms of mass prescriptions issued by an educational or esoteric elite which justifies those prescriptions on the basis of the "best for the most" fallacy. Bruce Joyce blames curriculum specialists in part for the tendency of schools to force collective prescriptions onto students: "Curriculum specialists of all types do have one thing in common: they have been co-opted into the service of a bureaucratic, monolithic, largely dehumanized educational system and unless they change their orientations radically they will be unable to work for humanistic ends."[14]

The radical model of education emphasizes that each individual should attempt to develop his fullest potential. This model does not demand immediate homogenization of knowledge and people. Indeed, the "melting pot" objective and assimilation are quite foreign to radical aims. Rather, the activists advocate the adoption of a systematic effort to cultivate the various cultural, ethnic, and individual contributions to art and knowledge. The error of certain "democrats," according to some of the more radical activists, is that they have regarded assimilation as the only means of achieving social tranquility. Radicals emphasize the need for pluralism, whereas "liberals" strive for a society based upon compromise, assimilation, and majority opinion on political matters.

Many student activists state that they prefer an educational experience which does not stress "professionalization" at the expense of "education." The universities, they say, should not be operated mainly as training grounds for professionals and technicians. When teaching is reduced to the level of training to meet the standards of professionalism, and when research is geared merely to the needs of professors to publish and gain stature within the university, students as learners cannot help but be overlooked.[15] According to the activists, forms of education that function to perpetuate an oligarchic community of nepotistic academics should be discouraged.

If the activists had their way, the school environment would be freed from the oppressive power of "professionals" who constitute one of the main blocks against fundamental change in education. The following malpractices of so-called professionals would also cease: falsely persuading the public to believe that the school has some valuable service to offer when it has none; perpetuating practices which rely upon hoodwinking and manipulating students rather than developing programs which would truly assist them in leading happier and more successful lives; taking unfair advantage of a captive audience, including extracting high wages for necessary but trivial services; engaging in activities which are self-enhancing for the "professional" but which serve no useful public function; withholding valuable information from students; misusing knowledge gained as a result of differential access to information; and holding monopolies on the dispensation of vital services when no need for the monopoly exists.

Some of these seemingly logical demands are regarded as totally unacceptable by certain educators who regard the activists as "destructive anarchists." But some students have become almost incapable of enduring this paternalistic attitude. It will only antagonize a student radical to tell him that he is acting like a child and that his demands are totally unreasonable. The radical activist is increasingly suspect of invitations to participate in any decision-making process that only functions to perpetuate present conditions. He believes that this process usually allows only token change. Activists usually wish to change institutions themselves, rather than minor processes within those institutions.

THE JESUS MOVEMENT

In Toronto a large group of young people known as the Catacomb Club meets each Thursday evening and Sunday afternoon. The Catacombs started at a Scarborough high school in 1968 when two high school students approached the head of their music department and asked him to sponsor a prayer group—one which would prove more active and dynamic than previous groups such as Campus Life and the Salvation Army. At first the school's administration seemed apprehensive about allowing prayer meetings in the school. The group was forced to call itself a "history club" rather than a prayer group, and had to meet in the basement of the school. Thus the name "Catacombs" was adopted and has been retained up to the present day.

In June, 1969, the Catacomb Club began meeting in homes, and until autumn of 1970 its membership held at about forty. Later the group moved to a farm north of Toronto but returned to houses in the city as growth made space critical. Late in the winter the Catacomb Club was given space in Bathurst Street United Church, and quickly the number of regular attenders jumped to eight hundred. After a Catacombs-sponsored Power and Praise Festival in May 1971, the numbers mushroomed again. Leaders at the Catacombs considered the festival to be the largest single turning point in the Toronto Jesus movement, as thousands of people claimed to be "touched by the love of God."

As space became critical in October 1971, Saint Paul's Anglican Church, with a seating capacity of 3,600, invited the Catacombs to use their facilities. By this time many subgroup meetings were taking place in addition to regular weekly events. By August 1972 the group had formed a corporation to handle audio/visual evangelism, videotape production, cassette teaching, and book distribution. At the present time 3,000 people are involved in the club.

Although opposed to much of what takes place in school and society, the members of the Catacombs, like most Jesus people, do not attempt a revolution of socioeconomic systems. Nor do they seek to overthrow any political power. "Our revolution can, however, drastically alter any government rule by changing individual peoples' lives" claimed Donald Prossiter, one of the regular attenders.

The Catacombs, like most Jesus movement groups, makes no membership appeals, asks nothing from those who attend the meetings, and has no denominational affiliation. No offerings are taken and no constitution has been written. Forms of worship at the Catacombs are constantly changing, but every event is marked by freedom and spontaneity of song, prayer, and praise. The Catacomb Club is a "nonorganization" which depends upon free will offerings and free participation by those who wish to attend. Prossiter states that their only concern is "spreading the good news about Jesus and filling the kingdom of heaven with children of God." Groups similar to the Catacombs are now to be found in most Canadian and American cities.

Jesus People, Street People, and Jesus Freaks qualify for special consideration as dissenters because they are so numerous, vociferous, and aggressive in advocating societal reform. Jesus Freaks are especially countercultural in that they are adamantly opposed to many dominant themes and generally accepted practices in majority society. Jesus Freaks have stated that, in addition to being religious, they are anti-materialistic and opposed to dominant society's technostructure because of its "soul-destroying" character.

The Jesus revolution rejects not only the material values of conventional America but the prevailing wisdom of American theology. Success often means an impersonal and despiritualized life that increasingly finds release in sexploration, status, alcohol and conspicuous consumption. Christianity— or at least the brand of it preached in prestige seminaries, pulpits and church offices over recent decades—has emphasized an immanent God of nature and social movement, not the new movement's transcendental, personal God who comes to earth in the person of Jesus, in the lives of individuals, in miracles. The Jesus revolution, in short, is one that denies the virtues of the Secular City and heaps scorn on the message that God was ever dead.[16]

Jesus Freaks find their appeal mainly among the poor, the oppressed, the deviant, and the underprivileged people of society. Jesus People are "straight" compared to Jesus Freaks, who many times do not belong to any established churches. The Jesus Freaks are more opposed than the Jesus People to the "strangling tentacles of monolithic, ecclesiastical bureaucracy."

Jesus Freaks, Jesus People, and Street People are the three main components of the entire Jesus movement. Related to these groups are the Catholic Pentecostals who, according to one estimate, probably number over one million in North America. The emphasis in each of these new religious movements is on "living in the spirit" and "liberating people" in terms of their "spiritual potential." Similar emphases are to be found among the millions of followers of Zen Buddhism, Hare Krishna, and other mystical or religious teachings which view man as having a soul. Soul is defined as that "essence of man that transcends the physical or material world." Proponents of these religious beliefs claim that man is more than a citizen of this world as represented in the here and now. Man is also "a child of the universe" and is capable of participating as an individual in the life of the spirit. The Jesus People believe that as a citizen, man lives in time; society lives in time. In eternity, in timelessness, only the individual exists—there his existence is fixed, not in the sight of society but in the sight of God.

The Jesus People, Jesus Freaks, Street People, and Catholic Pentecostals are united by their faith in Christ. They feel that Christ was more than a human prophet. Jesus People proclaim that Christ was the actual Son of God and the Savior of the world. Jesus People wish not only to emulate the person of Christ—they claim that Christ lives within them and that Christ is the person who saves and sustains them. Their beliefs revolve around the necessity for an intense personal relationship with Christ, and the conviction that such a relationship should characterize every human life.

Jesus People movements are growing everywhere. Christian coffee houses, prayer communities, newspapers, and communes are springing up in many parts of North America. For an account of this trend read *Jesus People Come Alive*.[17] It is almost impossible to spend much time in the heart of any major Canadian city without at least once coming into contact with a Jesus Freak who may ask you a question like, "Brother, have you heard the Word?"

The Jesus Movement does not necessarily reject the traditional church but attempts to go beyond it. The Jesus Movement has moved forward at an almost unbelievable rate. Key spokesmen for the movement, such as David Wilkerson, have had an enormous effect. Wilkerson has organized over two hundred "teen challenge centres." His book, *The Cross and the Switchblade*, has sold over seven million copies and was also made into a movie.[18] On the west coast of the United States and Canada, the circulation of Jesus People newspapers rocketed to five hundred thousand per month. This Jesus People press serves as an instrument for tying the whole hip-Christian scene together. Jesus People in Toronto assisted in producing the *Hollywood Free Paper* and produce two other newspapers themselves, one of which is the widely distributed *Marantha*. Vancouver Jesus People produce a paper called *Smile—God Loves You*. The total effect of the Jesus Movement probably surpasses the effect of any other single protest movement on the North American scene, with the exception of the Black Protest Movement.

As a result of the Jesus Movement, teachers are likely to run across more and more Jesus people in their schools during the next few years. In Kingston, Ontario, the high school Jesus Movement was just emerging in 1973. After a Jesus festival in late 1972, featuring a speaker from London, Ontario, called Terry Sheppard, prayer groups started meeting daily before classes at one Kingston high school. Indications are that such groups will continue to grow in size and influence as did the Catacombs Club in Toronto. As their numbers grow, Jesus People will become more confident in terms of approaching potential converts. If the American pattern is followed in Canada, contacts between activist Jesus People and other students and educational authorities can be expected to increase during the seventies.

SUMMARY

Although the student activist movement has been cooling down, many vociferous student dissenters still remain. Dissent has not disappeared, even though the style of the dissenter has changed. Some of the student activists are good scholars and highly intelligent critics of the educational system. However, many creative students have left school in frustration. Responsible educators should remain sensitive to the reasons for student dissent. When student protest is responsible and likely to assist in bringing about constructive change, teachers, parents, and administrators should probably support the students. Student effort should be viewed as one means by which an inert, uncreative school system can be changed.

NOTES

1. Kenneth Keniston, "The Sources of Student Dissent," *Journal of Social Issues* 23 (1967): 108–37.

2. Dick Kleiner, "Students Would Rather Read Than Riot," *Kingston Whig Standard*, March 16, 1972.

3. Eric Fromm, *The Sane Society* (New York: Fawcett World Library, 1955), p. 126; and T. B. Bottomore and M. Rubel, eds., *Karl Marx: Selected Writings in Sociology and Social Philosophy* (London: C. A. Watts, 1961).

4. J. S. Kunen, *The Strawberry Statement: Notes of a High School Revolutionary* (New York: Random House, 1968); Kurt Vonnegut, Jr., *Our Time Is Now* (New York: Praeger, 1970); Tim and Julyan Reid, *Student Power and the Canadian Campus* (Toronto: Peter Martin, 1969); Marc Libarle and Tom Seglison, *High School Revolutionaries* (New York: Random Press, 1971); Gerald McGuigan, *Student Protest* (Toronto: Methuen, 1968); and Dimitrios J. Roussopoulos, *The New Left in Canada* (Montreal: Our Generation Press, 1970).

5. Kenneth Fish, *Conflict and Dissent in the High School* (Toronto: Collier-Macmillan, 1970).

6. Kenneth Fish, *Conflict and Dissent in the High School*, pp. 8–9. Copyright © 1970, The Bruce Publishing Company. Reprinted by permission of the Macmillan Company.

7. Charles Hampden-Turner, *Radical Man: The Process of Psycho-Social Development* (Cambridge, Mass.: Schenkman Publishing Company, 1970), p. 377. Reprinted by permission of the publisher.

8. McGuigan, *Student Protest*, pp. 13–49.

9. Charles Hampden-Turner and Philip Whitten, "Morals: Left and Right," *Psychology Today*, April 1971, pp. 39–43, 74, 76.

10. Charles A. Reich, *The Greening of America* (Toronto: Bantam Books, 1971), pp. 241–51. Reprinted by permission of the author.

11. R. M. Merelman, "The Development of Political Ideology: A Framework for the Analysis of Political Socialization," *American Political Science Review* 63, no. 3 (1969): 750–67.

12. Richard Flacks, "The Liberated Generation: An Exploration of the Roots of Student Protest," *Journal of Social Issues* 23 (1967): 52–75; and Kenneth Keniston, *Young Radicals: Notes on Committed Youth* (New York: Harcourt, Brace & World, 1968).

13. Joel Loken, Some Correlates of Alienation, Master's thesis, University of Calgary, 1968; and Joel Loken, "Allocentrism and Activism," paper given at the Learning Research Faculty Seminar, Queen's University, December 1972.

14. Bruce Joyce, "Curriculum and Humanistic Education: Monolism vs. Pluralism," in *Humanistic Foundations*, ed. Carl Weinberg (Englewood Cliffs, N.J.: Prentice-Hall, 1972), p. 172.

15. Louis Kampf, "The Radical Faculty," *The Humanist*, November-December 1969, pp. 9–10.

16. "The New Rebel Cry: Jesus Is Coming," *TIME*, June 21, 1971, p. 36. Reprinted by permission from *TIME, The Weekly Newsmagazine*; copyright Time Inc., 1971.

17. Walker L. Knight, *Jesus People Come Alive* (Wheaton, Ill.: Tyndale House, 1971).

18. David Wilkerson, *The Cross and the Switchblade* (New York: Pyramid Publications, 1963).

BIBLIOGRAPHY

Baird, Leonard L. "Who Protests? A Study of Student Activists," in Julian Foster and Durward Long, eds. *Protest! Student Activism in America.* New York: William Morrow & Co., 1970.

Bay, Christian. "Political and Apolitical Students." *Journal of Social Issues*, vol. 23, no. 3, 1967.

Cockburn, Alexander, and Robin Blackburn, eds. *Student Power: Problems, Diagnosis, Action.* Harmondsworth, England: Penguin Books, 1969.

Coles, Robert. *Children of Crisis.* Boston: Little & Brown, 1967.

Dunlap, Riley. "Radical and Conservative Student Activists: A Comparison of Family Backgrounds." *Pacific Sociological Review* 13, (Summer 1970): 171–81.

Fairfield, Roy P. "Voices through the Mortar: The High School Underground Speaks." In *Humanistic Frontiers in American Education.* Toronto: Prentice-Hall, 1971.

Halleck, S. L. "Hypotheses of Student Unrest." *Phi Delta Kappan,* September 1968.

Harder, Mary White; James T. Richardson; and Robert Simmonds. "Jesus People." *Psychology Today,* December 1972.

Heist, Paul. "The Dynamics of Student Discontent and Protest." Paper given at the Annual Meeting of the American Psychological Association, New York, 1966.

Hendrick, Irving G., and Reginald L. Jones. *Student Dissent in the Schools.* Boston: Houghton Mifflin, 1972.

Hunt, Jane. "Principals Report on Student Protest." *Education Digest,* December 1969.

Keniston, Kenneth. "The Sources of Student Dissent." *Journal of Social Sciences,* vol. 23, no. 3, 1967.

Kerpelman, Larry. "Student Political Activism and Ideology: Comparative Characteristics of Activists and Nonactivists." *Journal of Counseling Psychology,* vol. 16, no. 1, 1969.

Loken, Joel. "A Multivariate Analysis of Student Activism." Ph.D. dissertation, University of Alberta, 1970.

Marin, Peter. "The Fiery Vehemence of Youth." *The Centre Magazine,* January 1969.

Plowman, Edward E. *The Jesus Movement in America.* Elgin, Ill.: David C. Cook Publishing Co., 1971.

Postman, Neil, and Charles Weingartner. *Teaching as a Subversive Activity.* New York: Delacorte Press, 1969.

Quarter, Jack. *The Student Movement of the 60s.* Toronto: Ontario Institute for Studies in Education, 1972.

Roszak, Theodore. *The Making of a Counter Culture.* Doubleday Anchor Press, 1969.

Rush, Gary B. "The Radicalism of Middle Class Youth." Presented at the Seventh World Congress of Sociology, Varma, Bulgaria, 1970. Available from Simon Fraser University, Burnaby, British Columbia.

Schachtel, Ernest. *Metamorphosis.* New York: Basic Books, 1959.

Szwaja, Lynn; Susan Pennybacker; Laurie Sandon; Joe Pickering; and Sharon Matthews. "High School Activists Tell What They Want." *Nation's Schools* vol. 84, 1964.

Thomson, Scott D. "Activism: A Game for Unloving Critics." *Education Digest*, September 1969.

Westhues, Kenneth. "Contrasting Biases of Research on the Youth Scene, 1960–70." Paper presented at the Annual Meeting of Western Sociological Association, Calgary, December 1971.

4 Change and confrontation

We innovate and renovate, and beneath it all, our schemes
always contain the same vacancies, the same smells of death, as
the schools. One speaks of planners, designers, teachers, and
administrators; one hears about schedules and modules, and
curricular innovation—new systems. It is always "materials" and
"technique," the chronic American technological vice, the
cure that murders as it saves. It is all so smug, so progressively
right—and yet so useless, so far off the track. One knows there
is something else altogether: a way of feeling, access to the
soul, a way of speaking and embracing, that lies at the heart of
all yearning or wisdom or real revolution. It is that, precisely,
that has been left out. It is something the planners cannot
remember: the living tissue of community. Without it, of course,
we shrivel and die, but who can speak convincingly about
that to those who have never felt it?[1]

RADICAL STUDENTS are probably correct in their assessment that schools
have become ritualistic conveyors of much obsolete information.
Students and teachers have been co-opted involuntarily in this process
and sometimes feel powerless to do anything to change the system.
Attendance requirements, grades, curriculum content, treatment of
students, time assigned to various courses, choices, working conditions,
teaching methods, and school regulations are only a few of the things
that need to be remodelled. These things need to be altered drastically,
contrary to what the moderate liberal reformists seem to believe. A
deep, thoroughgoing change of the entire system is necessary if the
school is to cease alienating students and begin to educate them
responsibly.

Some "innovative" educators have preferred to think that students
are increasingly satisfied because their schools are becoming more
"democratic," "open," and "free." The fact is that schools are still

59

impersonal, overcrowded, and understaffed. Consequently many students still consider school a "bummer." Certain sociological data suggest that "innovative" school systems may be real disaster areas; Diane Divoky reports that "no other school system has absorbed so many programs as New York, and yet is so obsolete today."[2] One of the reasons for this discouraging situation is that innovations which have been introduced have done little to solve the really big problems—depersonalization and the students' feeling of powerlessness. The present dilemma may be partially described by the following statement:

Priorities of the rule-makers (teachers, officials)

priorities of the rule-benefactors (students)

The result of this discrepancy is that many of the most intelligent students are bored out of their minds. Educational innovation hasn't basically changed this boredom. We have knocked down some of the interior walls and described those schools as being "open concept." Certain classes were combined and it was called "team teaching." Team teaching sometimes meant that two or more classes could be taught in one space, at one time, by one teacher while other teachers went for coffee. Students are given teaching machines, individual timetabling, modular schedules, and more "free time." All this is termed "individually prescribed programming." One thing hasn't changed—that is, the depersonalization which results from too little student-teacher contact and groups that are too large and unwieldy to accommodate small-group discussion and activity. Rather than implementing administrative and technological innovation, schools now require the kind of humanistic innovation which would facilitate and improve the student/teacher, student/student, and teacher/teacher relations.

THE CYCLE OF CONFLICT

Historians have shown sociologists that there are clearly delineated stages in the change process. Some historians believe that certain kinds of conflict are also cyclic; that is, they continually recur in history. A model is presented of stages that may occur in the "cycle of conflict." Although some conflict exists in each stage, the conflict at certain points in the cycle is much less overt than in others. The type of conflict engendered as a powerful group attempts to consolidate its influence (Stage 1) is different from the type of conflict resulting from the challenge of an emergent group of radicals who challenge well-established power (Stage 2).

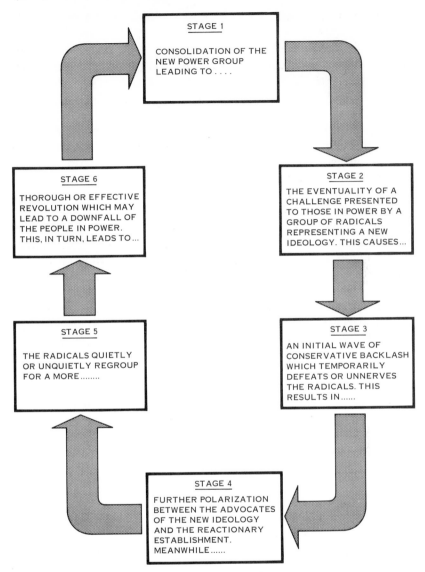

The Cycle of Conflict

In seeking to ascertain the stage of conflict the educational system is experiencing today, the sociologist must consider the entire cycle of change and try to determine what stages have already taken place. Many educational sociologists feel that during the last fifteen years the educational system has been passing through the second, third, and fourth stages described in the model. In the universities, we have seen the completion of an initial wave of rebellious protests (Stage

3) which were designed by radicals to "'liberate" and "humanize" the educational system. We have also witnessed the first strong wave of reaction to the student rebellion (Stage 4). In the meantime many radicals and revolutionaries are thought to be planning new strategies for change (Stage 5).

CONFRONTATIONS

Examinations of specific conflict situations involving some kind of actual confrontation between educators and student dissenters may assist us in understanding some of the usual reasons for the conflict. We shall see that the differing points of view held by students and the educational authorities confirm what Hannah Arendt has said about the tendency of opponents to hold stereotyped views of one another.[3] These stereotypes are sometimes at least partially responsible for the development of conflict. Arendt states that radicals often view the existing power structures as inefficient, stupid, corrupt, oppressive, self-concerned, and inflexible. Administrators are sometimes seen as dishonest, manipulating tyrants who do not respect the freedom and the dignity of students. On the other hand, educational leaders embroiled in conflicts sometimes think of the student revolutionaries as cunningly dangerous and hopelessly idealistic. Radicals are sometimes typecast as neurotic and irresponsible. They are seen as jealous of those in power and are also regarded as having other personality problems.

The student revolutionaries sometimes charge that the entire educational process is geared to the wishes of an elite. The educational elite is viewed as serving itself. The present administration is considered to be representative of society's landlords (who come disproportionately from one ethnic group and a particular social class). The administration states that "even if there is an elite, it knows best," and that in the interests of maintaining "educational standards" it must remain in power. The usual defence of the administration is "We may not be perfect, but we're efficient!"

The administration may reduce its oppressive policies or introduce more liberal policies for the school. However, no halfway changes or token reforms on the part of school authorities are usually accepted by the student revolutionaries because this would constitute a sell-out or a compromised bargain. Antagonism between the administration and the revolutionaries may continue unsolved for any length of time. Each side claims certain victories. Myths and legends are created in both camps. Charges and countercharges are laid. The revolutionary discredits as false propaganda, information given by the administration. Sometimes untrue stories are circulated about the people most involved. For a major breakthrough to occur, the administration must make some timely mistakes. Sometimes its own inconsistency or demoralization may make it possible for the radicals to gain public support. More often the students overreact or lose the support of other students as a result of their public image of destructive idealists.

The role of "Joe average" student is still considered to be important in influencing the final outcomes of a school conflict situation. It is the ordinary student who will swing the odds in one direction or another. In many cases it is impossible for the radical students who are aware of the problems to relate to the entire student body. Increasingly, the radical alienation of the more intelligent students has involved their shocking repudiation of the whole society in which they live. This revulsion of society is no more directed toward oligarchies and elite administrators than it is toward "straights," "liberals," teachers, parents, and most of the norms and values of society itself. Several of these generalizations are confirmed by the case study which follows.

CONFRONTATION IN AN URBAN SCHOOL—FAIRVIEW[4]

Fairview's Behavioral Objectives. Since before World War II Fairview had a cluster of values associated with it. One could safely say that these values had been perpetuated by past school administrations. It is more difficult to determine how these values originated; that is, whether the administrators had articulated such values in answer to specific needs, or whether they actually determined the needs. Nevertheless, at the time of the crisis, there was a conscious attempt on the part of Fairview's administration to maintain these values as though they were sacred by virtue of tradition or longevity. It was also noticeable, during the crisis, that the teaching staff was definitely acting in the role of inculcator of these values. In fact, individual teachers were evaluated in terms of their effectiveness and ability in implementing these traditional values.

Foremost among these values was that education at the secondary school level should be a pre-university training program, and that (as a corollary to the first) the student should be quiescent in doing what the teachers wanted or demanded. The school catered to students from middle class and professional backgrounds. Therefore, dress was seen as an indicator of taste and social standing, and only certain forms of dress were tolerated. In addition, certain forms of behavior and attitude were expected and maintained rigorously by the staff and administration for all its students. This resulted in a certain homogeneity among the staff and students alike. Such discipline was intended to adequately prepare students for a post-secondary future that was static and traditional in its demands. Every aspect of the school was permeated with corollaries or variables of the central values of the school. Reinforced by a high standard of past academic achievement, the staff felt that only certain methods in teaching/learning would work, and that excellence in school had some mystical relation to excellence of character.

Little evidence can be provided to show that, until the confrontation about to be discussed, these traditional values had ever been seriously or openly challenged by anyone. I say "seriously" and "openly" advisedly, because the staff members who did not fit in with these values were not hired back after the first year at Fairview. Students who proved too difficult to be dealt with through the normal channels of discipline were encouraged to transfer to another school. The school's record of scholarships, grades, and awards shows that the school's training was beneficial to those graduates from the school who went on to universities. This evidence tended to reinforce the educational philosophy of the school's officials and teachers. One must say that many students profited from what Fairview was doing.

It was the administration's refusal to deal realistically with the seeds of discontent that triggered the chain of reactions about to be described. Communication channels in the school constituted a one-way system in which the staff always won. Student government was subtly managed by the administration. Since little open dissent and debate were allowed, subversion became the necessary manner of attack. The eventual revolt was created as much by school officials as anyone else.

A major issue in the controversy was the fact that too much attention was paid to producing a certain type of scholar. The process leading to "scholarliness" was predetermined, unquestioned, and forcibly maintained. Any student's progress was measured in terms of the school's criterion of scholarliness. Deviations from this "standard of excellence" were dealt with in an authoritarian and dogmatic way by teachers and administrators alike. Such attitudes resulted in a fixed style of classroom teaching that one could characterize as oppressive to many students. Teachers became dogmatic and zealous in mastering effective means to an end that seemed to be incompatible with the real needs of the students.

The goals of the school were aided by the parents of students attending the school. These parents were interested in post-secondary education for their children, not only because of their experience in business, but also because the reputation of the school was such that attendance was practically a guarantee of future success. So parents of students reinforced the values of the school. For instance, school discipline problems were initially handled by the school and later dealt with and backed up by the concerned parents. Because of the similarity of values held by the families and the school, Fairview's staff and administration seemed comfortable in carrying out their traditional teaching objectives. Little did they know that some students were organizing to confront and disturb that comfort.

Attitudes of the Staff. Before proceeding to the confrontation, it might be helpful to describe the staff in more detail. The staff felt that the atmosphere in the school and their methods of teaching were generally satisfactory to the students. Most of the staff members were products of an educational system similar to that at Fairview. The principal made much of the fact that many of his former students returned as teachers. Former students were always hired in preference to teachers who had not attended Fairview. The teaching staff was not aware of the deep feelings of anger and resentment against the schooling/teaching which were felt by a small group of activists.

The teachers unconsciously reinforced their value systems. For instance, much of the staff room conversation centred upon proving that one could handle his/her job including the toughest discipline cases. This "image-projecting" activity was probably a defensive measure against discussion of teaching techniques or aims. Partly because of their unwillingness to examine what was actually going on in their students' heads, the teachers tended to believe that dissent was a straightforward discipline problem rather than a reaction to their role as information disseminators and manipulators. As they tended to think in terms of stereotypes and collective groups, they missed the exceptions to the standard. Working in conjunction with this stereotyping of students and homogenization of aims was a particular attitude regarding what constituted good teaching. This attitude developed as a natural response to the demanding standard of teacher effectiveness and evaluation expected by the central office. "Image-projecting" and a heightened sense of the importance of administrative minutiae therefore became all-important; teachers became increasingly involved in the maintenance of strict order in non-teaching matters (such as hall patrols, dress codes and study hall quiet), and in tight discipline in the teaching situation. The teachers' dominance was evidenced in their questioning techniques, project approaches, and assignments.

Little staff dissent was tolerated at Fairview and there was a low level of acceptance for alternatives or heterogeneous attitudes. It is my opinion that this lack of pluralism reflects a serious anti-democratic tendency that is frustrating to many students. Anti-pluralism and "loyalty" to "staff line" were so powerful that the younger teachers were terrified to challenge it, even though they realized that the school's biases were clearly opposite to the majority of students. Staff discipline was as tight as student discipline.

Values of the Activists. Foremost among the values of the activists was a romantic, but earnestly felt, desire to achieve self-expression. This self-expression was to be measured in terms not bounded by conventional restraints on feeling, initiative, and communication. Related to this value was a firm anti-authoritarianism or antipathy toward arbitrary rule and centralized decision making. These values were amplified by the obstinacy of the teachers and administrators. The activists' romanticism and anti-authoritarianism led to a strong belief in students' abilities to share the leadership in determining their activities. This value could be described as a kind of elitism, in that most activists felt that their student group was better equipped to lead than those in power. Also, fundamental in the activists' value system was a supposed anti-dogmatism, a rejection of the administration's ideologies and the institutionalist nature of the education offered in terms of those ideologies. The activists wanted to replace one form of dogmatism with another, and one form of institutional hierarchy with another. Such "either/or" solutions really are not effective. But the activists' beliefs had been unchallenged because the system of disciplining at the school touched only the peripheries of the activists' complaints.

I would like to emphasize that the tenor of the activists' thinking was established long before the confrontation actually happened and it only became more extreme during the crisis. In many ways the activitists were forced into a strident position, but they allowed themselves to be forced into it. In a sense, the activists stopped thinking and began to emote. They stopped being "radical" and became "fascist." They became so frustrated and enraged with school policies that they stopped being functional and pragmatic. Furthermore, the radicals believed that only their own methods were correct; hence, they exhibited the most inflexible form of radical thinking, a passionately held viewpoint in which reasoning played little part. Furthermore, the activitists became over-conscious of their own dramatic role in the conflict and they made a deliberate attempt to manipulate others in terms of their own goals. Such "radical chic" politics (current "hip" radicalism) are characterized by sloganeering, "we-they" conspiracy theories, deliberate and irrational polarization of groups into black-white alternative structures, and anti-intellectual and unintelligent statements or actions. I believe that the truly "radical" person is one who constantly analyses and reanalyses his own as well as his opponents' ways of thinking, assumptions, and programs.

The Confrontation. The controversy had opened on the question of student government or, more specifically, the ability of the students to elect their own representatives without having them screened by the administration in terms of desire to co-operate with the central office in carrying out the fundamental aims and values of the school. The administration traditionally approved nominations and read the election speeches before they were delivered to the student assembly. A small group of students were angered at this infringement of their rights.

They also suspected that the student council represented only the "pro-school" personalities, so this small group of radicals decided to ridicule and satirize the whole election procedure. Their method was to plaster the school before nomination week with posters and bumper-stickers announcing the candidacy of "Kenny Lingus" (a bastardized anglicization of the Latin, *cunnilingus*). The staff was slow to even realize what the name implied until the principal, an old Latin teacher, explained.

Tactics of the Activists.   Before discussing the consequences of these actions, it would be useful to analyse the tactics used by the activists. What separated the activists from other student dissenters, such as the delinquents, were their methods of confrontation. Whereas the delinquents purposely went out of their way to disturb the staff, the activists firmly believed that, through a comic, insulting, devious slander campaign, they could invigorate student opinion to their side and compel the staff to change. It is important to realize that the activists wanted changes in line with their own preferences and the means to be used were their own preferred means.

In solving a confrontation crisis, it is important to determine what methods of confrontation are being used. If one is able to determine the nature of the confrontation, one can almost certainly predict the nature of events that will follow. If there is an honest attempt by the antagonists to rationally and nonviolently generate alternatives, then the teachers might act in conjunction with the students (despite fears that things will blow up!). If the original confrontation is irrational, dogmatically pronounced, and arrogantly adhered to, then the opposing group will destroy their opponents' characters and arguments, and the crisis will escalate. If the original confrontation is one of insincere tricksterism, the educational authorities might react by ignoring the students' demands. Too often, what has happened is that the student radicals are regarded as arrogant children and treated as such. Most confrontations have the potential to teach both parties something.

Radical students should realize that it does no good to kick a man in the face, burn his buildings, urinate in his driveway, and then turn to him and say, "Wake up. Truth is here!" This violent form of confrontation is passé. Some confrontation leads to a very unnecessary polarization in which it is very difficult to get one group to moderate its position and engage in concrete discussions. The activists at Fairview confronted the teachers in an openly ridiculing way. Inadvertently they reinforced every prejudice about radicals which was held by teachers at the school. Some teachers felt concerned about the students, but most were playing a game they had already played many times before—poker, with five aces. The staff couldn't afford to lose. They would have, if the methods of the activists had educated the staff rather than reconvincing them of their own values. The "staff line" and "loyalty to the boss" won out; conditioned response and vested interest met conditioned response and vested interest.

Consequences of the Activists' Tactics.   What had to be regretted in the Fairview situation was not the fact that the activists chose the wrong type of confrontation, but rather that there was a confrontation at all. Confrontation was altogether unnecessary. The administration and staff had unflinchingly imposed their own system of values and methods of discipline. The activists' resentments built up to the point where their eventual response turned out to be childlike: malicious, vindictive, arrogant, and irrational. However, the staff reactions were also questionable. Dogmatic attitudes toward standards and values were apparent in lectures given by certain staff members in their classes. Students who were "pro-school" were encouraged to "talk" with the activists. The activists reacted in even more subversive ways. The activists' answer was an underground newspaper which carried over the arguments involving the elections in even stronger terms.

The activists' newspaper provoked the administration's restatement of the Fairview catechism. The activists were singled out as delinquents, penalized and treated as a subversive group. Their powers to vote were taken away temporarily. The elections were held and a "pro-school" slate of candidates was elected.

Eventually, the principal decided to leave the activists alone. However, a group of teachers decided that more extreme measures were required. The result was an attack mounted in these teachers' classes on the paper's editorial board, more "pro-school" students' "talk sessions," and a desire to curtail all extracurricular activities. Most of the teachers supported these measures.

As a result of staff involvement, a politicization of the delinquents and the apathetics occurred that was powerful in its antagonism toward the teachers, but as well toward the activists. The activists had no control over this group and, as a result, they were confronted by new opponents. The reasons for this new activity were twofold: the delinquents did not want to miss the fun and the apathetics were fed up with disruptions.

My "baptism by ordeal" started when I was asked to attend a

special staff meeting. After the meeting I was very hesitant to do what was demanded by the new "staff line." After talking to my wife, who shared my acute awareness of our dwindling bank account and my deep depression at the thought of moving the following year, I was even more hesitant. I slept little that night, but I left the next morning, conscious of my part in the developing act. I, quite frankly, was not thinking clearly at this time—probably because I was a product of Fairview as a student, believed in the values it stood for, and didn't know anything else. I'd just left graduate school at Queen's University where I'd been "jumping hoops" for so long that I didn't know who I was. All that meaningless involvement was about to change.

I started talking to a seminar of kids I had been really enjoying that year. We had been getting along quite well and great things had been happening. They had given me more than I had given them; they were reading a lot more than they ever had before, writing with power, and talking responsibly. It must have been quite a shock to them when I came in and talked like a goon spouting the staff line.

After I was through spouting the line, Mark, who was on my basketball team and also the assistant editor of the underground paper, started to talk very slowly and quietly. Then he started to get louder, and I suddenly realized that I was frightened of him, liked him, and respected him all at the same time. Then he started to get even louder. He ended up shouting. He sat down. I started to talk very slowly, then louder, and ended up shouting. I sat down. Mark started to cry. The bell rang. I cried. Mark and I just sat there and cried.

Mark and I got up after the other kids had left. He looked at me and asked why I, of all people, had not left him alone. In every one of his classes he was getting the "big line" and he was thinking of leaving school. I gave him my handkerchief, told him that I was an ass, that I was sorry, that I was irresponsible for doing what I did to him, and that I was thinking of resigning. We talked on the way to our next classes and decided to have lunch together. That conversation was the birth of my radicalization! It was the first time I'd had lunch with a student too. Not a big start, but a start.

Mark and I started the next day in our seminar and discussed the whole thing with the group. The obvious thing was to stop the escalation of the confrontation. But how? This was really the first time I'd talked with students, and it was frightening when I realized that I didn't know how. The students felt the same way talking with me, but somehow we managed. This was the first time any of us had tried to reason out alternatives and look for more radical solutions to what was ailing us and others.

Errors of the Activists. Mark and I agreed in retrospect that the activists had committed tactical errors—small perhaps, in comparison with the seminal stupidities of the administrators and staff, but big enough to destroy their own means and ends! By not radicalizing and politicizing the student body, the activists allowed the staff to politicize the students for their own needs and confront the activists. The teachers had the power to do this. The activists had failed to realize that they needed the larger power base of the students and their participation to achieve their ends, but their value of elitism hindered this. The fact that they did not accommodate these students led to their being confronted by "straights," delinquents, and apathetics as well as the staff; hence, their energies were displaced from the central focus of the confrontation.

Second, the activists suffered from a delusion about the real nature of power politics. They indulged in too much verbal theorizing and too little real analysis of their opponents' powers. It is not possible to call the administrators "paper tigers" and not have them react. The activists believed that polarization of staff versus activists would rally the rest of the students behind the activists. But this never happened. Most of the students who were the "pro-school types" felt threatened, and with the encouragement of their teachers they began to oppose the activists. The activists even failed to perceive that at the end of the confrontation they as students would have to work with the very people they had confronted, and that it was unrealistic to think otherwise. The activists had manipulated themselves into the position where they could not work with their fellow students or teachers. Consequently, the activists were not included in the post-confrontation negotiations. However, many of them left school after the crisis.

Implementation of Reforms. The new group presenting the alternatives was characterized by new values and assumptions. Foremost was that the present method of confrontation was idiotic, obscene, and unintelligent. Second was that, if any changes were to occur, they had to involve staff, administration, and students working together in a meaningful and effective way. Third was the assumption that the changes had to be functional, in the sense that they had to reinvigorate the institution and make it work—chaos is tiring! Fourth was that a central committee had to be established that consisted of representatives of all segments of the school. Fifth was the belief that this committee had to be supplemented and complemented by external organizations (such as the Student Council and Staff Assembly/Committees) in order that suggested programs be implemented and approved on a continuous evaluation procedure. Finally, the assumption was held that new dialogues between classroom teachers and students had to be opened up to accommodate dissent and changes.

With these assumptions and programs, a small group of staff and students went to the principal. The new program was voted upon by the Staff Assembly and Student Council, and passed unanimously in both places. Immediate plans were put into effect to implement the new program. Elections were held and several activists were elected. Other meetings began during that term and were carried into the next school year. As a result of these meetings, the following changes took place: independent study programs were implemented; the bells were removed; dress codes disappeared; "activity days" which sometimes replaced regular school classes were introduced for the first time; grade thirteen attendance became noncompulsory, and attendance in grades eleven and twelve became noncompulsory when an average of 60 percent was maintained; a school newspaper was established; a Staff-Student Academic Study Committee was established; and a more "liberal" attitude and atmosphere generally seemed to prevail.

CONFRONTATION IN A BILINGUAL SCHOOL

Introduction. The following account is based on a combination of ingredients which were found to characterize a student system confrontation which actually occurred. Cornwall and Sturgeon Falls, Ontario, are two communities that have experienced major conflicts related to the French-English language issue. However, Cornwall and Sturgeon Falls are not the communities referred to in this case study. It will become apparent that the reasons for student rebellion and administrative difficulties in some bicultural areas can be very complex. It is difficult to describe such conflict in such simplistic terms as student versus the school.

The Setting. The town in which the confrontation occurred has a population of nine thousand people and is located near the Quebec border in rural Ontario. The town serves as a business centre for the many farmers in the area. Eighty percent of the population of the area is French Canadian. Average socioeconomic conditions prevail among the inhabitants of the area. The local high school serves seven hundred students.

The staff at the school was evenly split between English and French Canadian teachers. Two of the school's thirty-odd teachers claimed to be French separatists. The principal was French Canadian but very conservative and antiseparatist. Twenty percent of the French Canadian students were thought to be separatist in their attitudes. French Canadian students made up ninety percent of the school's population.

Problems of the School. Before the major conflict began, the school faced several problems. Although constituted as a bilingual school, most of the classes were taught in English. This was regarded as unfair by most of the French students who felt that they had to compete with other students within the school and in the rest of the province, who were at an advantage because of their English language proficiency. Many of the French Canadian students spoke almost no English at all.

In addition to the language difficulties there was a student-teacher problem. Certain teachers were regarded as being incompetent. Their incompetence was attributed to them partly because they could not speak French. Some bilingual teachers were also considered incompetent. For instance, one elderly bilingual teacher was regarded competent in the mastery of her subject area but had real difficulties in communicating the content to her students. Another teacher was an alcoholic who frequently absented himself from school. The principal did not seem to be overly concerned about such problems. Many teachers, especially the newer ones, and many people in the community criticized the principal for failing to take any action against these teachers.

A third major problem faced by the school was that the students had inadequate recreational facilities. The school had no gymnasium or special student areas such as smoking rooms or lounges. An outdoor skating rink was open for about four months in the winter. The rink was the only sports facility available to students. In addition to the lack of sports facilities, students and staff members had very busy timetables. The reason for this was that students were required to take one additional subject beyond those required by the policies of the department of education. Students were to enrol in the extra subject as a safeguard against failing another course. The additional course load put an extra burden on students and teachers alike, some of whom never had any free periods.

Confrontation. The confrontation described should be viewed as a series of events rather than as a single showdown between dissident students and the administration. On one occasion the students all walked out of school. The reason for the walkout was that the administration had failed to act on policy changes demanded by the students. The students had asked, through a committee, that certain features of the new Ontario Department of Education H.S. 1 policies be implemented, such as removal of academic prerequisites for certain courses; removal of the school's rules making it necessary to enrol in certain "hard core" subjects; and removal of the necessity to register in one extra course beyond the usual requirements.

On another occasion, approximately half the students staged a demonstration in the schoolyard during the noon hour. A variety of issues were involved. These issues were referred to by signs carried by the demonstrators. Most of the signs demanded more French instruction, more bilingual teachers, and removal of obsolete rules. The separatist teachers evidently supported the students in their demands.

Conflict of another kind was also seen to exist in the school. Several French Canadian students became outwardly insolent and began engaging in a variety of delinquent behaviors. One French boy, Guy, was especially troublesome. He swore at his English teachers in French. He had a particularly difficult time with the elderly woman teacher who was mentioned earlier as having communication problems with her students. Guy was instrumental in instigating other students to engage in antischool activities. Many teachers regarded these actions as symptomatic of the fact that Guy was extremely frustrated because he could not speak English. Certain teachers had been very harsh in their criticism of Guy. One teacher went so far as to insult Guy's family in the course of reprimanding him for interrupting a lesson. Other students "acted up" but Guy was known throughout the school for his rebellious antics.

All the confrontational activities including the walkout, the demonstration, and the acts of delinquency were met with indecision by the administration. The situation continued to disintegrate until the school board finally took matters into its own hands.

Implementation of Reform. Once the board decided to act, certain reforms were swiftly introduced. The suddenness of the board's actions surprised everyone. The school's principal was dismissed, and a new principal took office. The guidance department was supplemented by the addition of two new counsellors. Certain teachers upon whom the student criticism had been focussed were also replaced. The teacher load was reduced by hiring several new teachers, and these new teachers were bilingual. The non-French-speaking teachers who remained at the school have been encouraged by the board to learn French as soon as possible. Grants are being made available to teachers who wish to study French during the summer months. More courses are now being taught in French. In addition, the more flexible H.S. 1 policies are being gradually phased in. Most students and teachers claim that there has been an almost unbelievable improvement in morale at the school. Student alienation and deliquency have been noticeably reduced. Incidentally, Guy was transferred to another school and is reported to be doing well. The board is planning to improve the students' recreational facilities; however, economic constraints still delay the building of the gymnasium.

DEALING WITH CONFLICT AND CHANGE

People who advocate basic change of any kind challenge and threaten our institutions. Some people who do not understand change and who view those who demand change as destructive are often made incompetent by fear. Those who are severely paralyzed by fear have a tendency to restrict themselves to immediate symptoms of change. This does little to alleviate the fundamental conditions which have led to the demand for change. Added to those who favor simplistic solutions are those who wish to exploit the concerns of individuals. These are the people who wish to gain fame and fortune by attaching themselves pretentiously to the "demand-for-change bandwagon."

Social scientists have done considerable study and research on controversy and conflict and are now in a position to make some recommendations to persons involved in the process of social change. The knowledge we have about conflict and how to deal with it should be translated to educators who are continually involved with dissent and demands for change.

Administrators can sometimes avoid polarization by attempting to keep controversies from becoming violent or destructive and by struggling to keep open the channels of communication between the antagonists. Administrators should enter conflicts not as partisans but in such a way that pressure is exerted on partisans to resolve their difficulties. "Conflict resolution specialists" point out to the partisans that many outcomes of the conflict are possible. One outcome is that both sides could gain *something*, without *completely satisfying* everyone. Another type of outcome is one in which people have been able to find a way to incorporate the goals of both sides in a creative new solution not previously anticipated. This process has been described by N. P. Follet in *Creative Experience.*[5]

Another related principle for resolving conflict has to do with *shared goals*. Groups may compete for certain ends but share goals at another level. Labour and management both may want good schools despite other differences. Ethnic groups may vie for position but share concern for health or other aspects of the community. Where mutually held goals can be identified and accepted, a lessening of competition or the threat of violence—a *functional correlation*—is apt to occur. This means collaboration only at the point of an operational interest or need. Catholics, Jews, and Protestants need not agree on creed in order to work together to keep a large industry from leaving the community.

Another thing to keep in mind is that before attempting to enter into a conflict situation the administrator must be sure of his facts.

One cannot make wise decisions without understanding fully what conditions have led to the conflict.

Finally, a widely developing point of view, or orientation toward controversy, is that of *nonviolence*. Following Gandhi, this viewpoint asserts that evil should not be ignored but should be confronted by resistance with no bitterness held against the opponent, but at the same time with no capitulation. The manner of confronting evil is through love and through suffering, if necessary; through receiving violence but never engaging in it. The theory is that anger produces anger, while *love produces love*. Sit-ins, the Freedom Riders, and protests against taking cover during civil defence drills all illustrate various modifications of the nonviolent approach.

One of the problems in handling controversy and conflict is that the specific situation one confronts usually calls for action more or less specifically designed to meet the key or central issues. Usually caution and understanding are required to determine just how to respond in a way that will lead to a sound solution.

● Before deciding how to react in a confrontation situation one should be sure of the actual importance of the issues raised.

● The conflict resolution specialist will need to consider the course and nature of the attack and the concerns and characteristics of the people directly involved.

● One should also consider the consequences of not doing something about an attack, recognizing that not acting may imply guilt or admit validity of the change.

● One should try to find what motivation lies behind the changes made and talk directly with the attackers where possible.

● Anyone who is trying to mediate a conflict between warring parties should develop and hold an attitude of reason and be careful to stick to the fundamental issues while keeping personalities out of the picture and employing criticism only as a constructive force.

SUMMARY

One of the fundamental issues in the student movement concerns student rights. Up until the late fifties, educators seemed to feel that students had few human rights. Schools were operated according to rules, regulations, and laws handed down by provincial departments of education, local school boards, and principals' offices. Students began questioning the educational authorities over a decade ago. When they were not heeded, the students took their demands one step further and staged walkouts, sit-ins, and demonstrations. Through constitutional as well as unconstitutional means, schools have been forced to make some changes in line with student preferences. Consequently student opinions and student participation have now become more important determinants of what happens in many schools.

NOTES

1. Peter Marin, "Children of the Apocalypse." Copyright © 1970 by Saturday Review, Inc. First appeared in *Saturday Review*, September 19, 1970, p. 73. Used with permission.

2. Diane Divoky, "New York's Mini-Schools: Small Miracles, Big Troubles," *Saturday Review*, December 18, 1971, p. 67.

3. Hannah Arendt, *On Revolution* (New York: The Viking Press, 1963), pp. 222–29.

4. The Fairview case study has been printed with the permission of the author, A. M. Gifford, Theatre Arts Department, College of Education, University of Toronto.

5. N. P. Follet, *Creative Experience* (New York: Peter Smith, 1951).

5 Educator response

Because of their lack of interaction with others and the "chosen" nature of their repudiation, alienated students are not easy to influence. Aspects of their alienation indicate that the isolation is real, and in some cases, irreversible. However, one must not conclude that alienation is necessarily and completely a negative quality. In spite of their hostility, dissent and impulsiveness, the alienated may have a real contribution to make. The creative ideas they generate could be channelled into a constructive reappraisal of society. Unorthodoxy challenges the status quo, and dissent does not necessarily have to be regarded as pathological. Frankness and emotional authenticity need not always offend. Beyond this, the intellectual motivation of the alienated is a positive quality.

SINCE THE ALIENATED STUDENT probably has difficulty living up to certain interpersonal demands, it may be wise to demand less of him in certain ways. He will not immediately enter into meaningful and constructive interaction with others. There are prerequisites to this in terms of his self-development. It is imperative for the instructor of the alienated student to establish authentic and emotionally open interpersonal contacts with him. Dealing with the alienated person merely on the basis of expediency will likely accentuate his condition. Instead the instructor must make a sincere attempt to relate to him as a full human being— as one with feeling, mentality, and understanding. The alienated student should be given opportunities to get involved, to test his self-image, to make decisions, to cooperate with others, to express himself, and to commit himself without fear of ridicule.

It is important to note in passing that true commitment does not emerge from package acceptance of an image or an idea created by the mass media. Sometimes this is forgotten. Commitment results from meaningful exposure to the basic issues at stake and the resulting decision of the individual to choose a place to stand. Often people are prone to perceive only the externals of purposefully projected images and in politics, for example, to seek out a magic, charismatic human savior to deliver them from their political and economic woes. This removes from them the responsibility of governing their own destinies. Such a "sell-out" of one's mentality leads to loss of human potential and the removal of integrity. This is becoming as true of the academic community as it is of the political or economic world.

Rather than being taught to accept predominant external images and values, pupils should be taught to formulate their own ideas. They should be encouraged to acknowledge their own feelings and thereby come to know themselves; that is, to develop a self-image. If they do not externalize important aspects of themselves but rather seek logical self-expression, they will develop healthier attitudes and more integrated personalities. This should be an educational objective.

It is possible to offend the alienated by presenting them with an ethic based merely on technology, or on values associated only with the economic status quo.[1] In short, the alien is attempting to overcome the technology. He frequently feels trapped in an inescapable, bureaucratic, and automated societal prison. It is possible for the teacher to perpetuate this feeling of powerlessness by maintaining an environment of scholastic ambiguity.

Scaling grades in such a way that the meaning of evaluation is not understood by the student is one way of maintaining his alienation. Unconsciously such methods are sometimes used to confuse the student so that he has no basis on which to make criticism of the prevailing situation. The instructor may operate this way because the very vitality and often misunderstood qualities of youth, and the alienated in particular, threaten him. Adults, rather than trying to understand, tend to erect impenetrable walls of defence to separate themselves from the source of anxiety—the student. A stereotype may function as such a wall. Administrative policy is frequently a useful sanctuary behind which the educator can hide. Furthermore, the education of an individual should not attempt to destroy his meaningful myths, fantasies, religious beliefs, convictions, intuitions, ideals, inspirations, or aesthetic expressions. This is precisely what a pragmatic, commercial, and cybernetic society tends to do. In this way our society has managed to alienate its original minority groups. If something could be put in the place of that which has been destroyed and consequently accepted by those being taught, the results of resocialization may not be catastrophic. But the present educational system lacks a coherent ideology or philosophy. As Keniston expressed it, our society lacks a vision of itself and of man that transcends technology.[2]

Instructors should not allow students to resign themselves to the trite, conventional, and mediocre. This is how dogmatic and simplistic thinking originates. Students should be encouraged to think intelligently about themselves as well as about the society in which they live. An excellent education should develop the individual's full potential. This is difficult to accomplish by the usual methods of educational mass production. The eccentricities and finer qualities of students tend to be overlooked in today's school. It may be that rebellion itself is a worthwhile quality. The alienated student should be taught to make his rebellion constructive.

Overly conventional thinking is frequently encouraged by attempts to coerce, proselytize, or force dogmatic thinking onto students. The effect is always alienating. It is important to realize that dogmatisms can be as easily pseudoscientific as puritan in origin. The school is as guilty as the Sunday school. Fundamentalism, which accompanies dogmatic thinking, is a state of mind as much as it is a religious phenomenon. The tragic fact is that all such thinking tends to betray authenticity and to prostitute human integrity.

Keniston expresses the opinion that the world is becoming somewhat inhuman because man has lost the capacity for dedication, concern, and whole-heartedness.[3] To be "human," in the total sense of the word, means to retain the capacity to love, hate, and experience other deep passions. To do so requires self-identity. The school may have had a detrimental effect by adopting the "melting pot" philosophy. In a melting pot, cultural identity, and with it, self-identity, tends to be irradicated. Yet the idea of the melting pot is still promoted in some social studies courses as an educational objective. The author suggests that the human problem today is not human diversity but human homogeneity which jeopardizes an individual's self-identity.

To be a man is to be what one is and not what one is expected to be. Consequently society must not deny the individual who insists on exhibiting the positive aspects of his self-identity the right to do so. In order for this to take place, it must become possible for all men to affirm themselves without fear of sanction.

If the problem of alienation is to be overcome, it is necessary to develop a new and shared criterion for social interaction based upon responsible individual behavior rather than upon legislation and legalism, which are becoming increasingly ineffective means of control. Youth must be prepared to shoulder adulthood by being taught to make responsible decisions and to renounce false dependency. Based upon this ethic of responsibility and a "new vision of a world beyond technology, success is possible."[4] Alienation and the search for identity can then be converted into legitimate and constructive aspirations.

Teachers may be interested to know that an innovative curriculum approach to the problem of alienation, including the general behavioral objectives and notes on teaching strategy, has been published by Bruce Joyce in *Humanistic Foundations of Education.*[5]

NOTES TO DISSENTING TEACHERS

Numerous teachers claim they cannot afford to be seen as openly rebellious, but that they are still in basic disagreement with the way schools are operated. Some teachers feel that officials of the secondary school system are still smug and unenlightened regarding the need for educational reform. Although dissenting teachers cannot afford to be outspoken, they have some reasons for encouragement.

When the dissenter is rejected by other educators, he need not abandon his hopes for change. He can appeal for validation of his opinions to respected educational authorities whose ideas are roughly the same as his own. The company of dissenters is remarkably distinguished and includes such notables as John Holt, A. S. Neill, Neil Postman, Ivan Illich, Dwight Allen, and Edgar Friedenberg. Many faculties of education now include more dissenters than ever before.

A second reason for encouragement exists. It does not take much intelligence to realize that there is a deep and enduring dissatisfaction, especially among high school students, but also among teachers, concerning the quality of education being offered in our public schools. Since standard approaches have made so little progress in solving the dilemma of the schools, it follows that the solution to these problems is probably radical. This radical solution probably lies outside the experience and imagination of most present educators. In fact, the ultimately successful solution would not be popular among school administrators of the present. Indeed, if the solution were immediately acceptable, it should probably be seriously questioned.

Dissenting teachers who are able to articulate alternatives which are ridiculed by their colleagues should be encouraged by the fact that their ideas are regarded with disdain and disbelief. One should be pleased that his dissent and life style are markedly different from those of educators who support the traditional school. Dissenters are sometimes most successful when they elicit strong feelings of derision and disagreement from the educational Establishment. Dissenters should take courage in the very fact that their ideas have not yet been tested—for the fact that the ideas have not been tested indicates that those ideas have not yet failed in practice.

However, at the same time that dissenters are encouraged in their ways they should realize that the Establishment will try to disparage and discredit them. The term "Establishment" does not refer to a centralized formal power structure, but a complex, composed of resistant and reactionary people who have a vested interest in the way things are. For instance, it is not always the principal of a school who holds back a creative or experimental teacher. More often, other more conventional teachers who resent the success or popularity of an inventive teacher may try to impede or inhibit him.

The Establishment can retaliate against the dissenter in several ways. It can label him an irresponsible, destructive deviant. The Establishment can regard the dissenter as a dreamer and clown who lacks any credibility. Accusing a person of being inconsistent or lacking in credibility is to disbelieve that his ideas are possible. The Establishment cannot believe that people who dissent are serious. The minute it does notice that a dissenter is serious, the Establishment takes effective actions to renounce him and reduce his influence. Consequently, the safest thing for a dissenter to do, especially when he is succeeding, is to establish his reputation as a failure.

Pierre Vallieres supports the notion about the Establishment's fear of competent dissenters. Vallieres was once a leading spokesman for the FLQ (Fédération de Libération du Québec). Now he has moderated his views and has shifted his support to the Parti Québécois. Speaking of the dissenter, Vallieres says:

> In the beginning your utopia makes some people pity you, others ridicule you, and the majority look upon you as a kind of mystic without God! It is not long before you have acquired a reputation for being a dreamer—a fellow who is "sincere" but "idealistic." If, on the top of that, you intend to go to action, then you become ipso facto a "communist," an "anarchist," an irresponsible and dangerous man who, in the interest of society, should be locked up as soon as possible in a prison or insane asylum. As long as you only preach your utopia, the established order is content to take note of your "dissent" with contempt or indifference. But as soon as you begin to act, the old system hastens to turn you into a public menace and a criminal so as to be able to bury you alive before your "idealism" puts Molotov cocktails, dynamite, and rifles in the hands of the workers and the young people.[6]

Of course, the revolutionary dissenter takes some action in spite of the fact that he knows the Establishment will take measures to scandalize him or render him ineffective. He knows that any act of courage will elicit similar acts of courage among other oppressed people and that the revolution will go on in the absence of his leadership. This feeling of dispensability is the hallmark of a successful dissenter. Dispensability might even be regarded by the dissenter as one way of immortalizing the effect of his dissent. Historically, the reactionary Establishment, no matter how hard it has tried, has never been able to eliminate men's souls. Dissent is sometimes an expression of soul in the face of a soulless society. At least the revolutionary chooses to think so.

Postman and Weingartner provided a handbook for changing schools. Hansen, Jensen, and Roberts have provided *The Little Red School Book*. By giving these books to students, the radical educator can indirectly exert pressure on the educational authorities and force them to change.[7] The intelligent thing to do seems to be to get the students working together for change. The technique of going to the students in a rational and nonmalicious way is contrary to the methods of "hard revolutionaries," who often utilize techniques which are destructive and often precipitate strongly negative reactions. Postman and Weingartner tell us that the "soft revolutionary" is a thoughtful, sensitive, and productive agent of change. He devises methods of playing the system against itself (the "judo technique"). Through learning to "detect bullshit," and by developing clever tactics of "dealing with crap," the radical learns to choose an effective course of subversion. The "soft revolutionary" is also capable of anticipating the counterrevolutionary responses of teachers and administrators who resist him.[8]

PHILOSOPHICAL DIFFERENCES AMONG EDUCATORS

It must be remembered that educators hold varying philosophies which govern how they respond to the cry for change. Some educators are sympathetic toward disenchanted students. Other educators are not. It is possible to analyse the assumptions and beliefs of educators keeping their differing philosophies in mind. First let us examine some of these differing philosophies and consider some of the educational implications of responding to educational problems within the context of those philosophies.

Right versus Left. First, it is essential to realize that there are serious ideological differences between educators. For instance educators of the Left and educators of the Right appear to be divided on their assumptions about human nature. These assumptions influence their perceptions of students and how many rights and privileges they should have. The issue has been called that of "faith in people". Nettler puts it aptly: "The Leftist thinks people are better than they are; the Rightist thinks they are worse."[9] The educator on the Left may think people (students) are basically honest and good. The educator on the Right may believe that people (students) are basically dishonest and prone to corruption if not constrained by school laws and regulations.

The Left believes that education should be provided fully to all who want it. The Right believes in rationing education; that it should be given only to those who will use and appreciate it. The educational policy maker's ideology is undoubtedly influential in determining who will be educated and who will not be educated. Generally the Left desires that government do more to educate people. The Right wants people to educate themselves, arguing that it is only in this way that they will regard education as worth while and appreciate it.

The Leftist tends to be a more permissive parent and educator; the Rightist believes in discipline and control. The Leftist, says Nettler, "encourages the expression of emotion, feeling, wish and dreams; the Rightist encourages reason, bounds and limits." The educational implications of these beliefs are obvious.

The Leftist believes that the government should control education because he believes that too much individual freedom has been the cause of the present educational dilemma. The Rightist believes that schools, like governments, should be operated with a minimum of interference by governments, rules, and regulations. Leftists rarely depoliticize education because, from their perspective, schools are places where collective responsibility should be taught.

Old Left versus New Left. It is naive to think that the conflict in the schools today is a simple reflection of the differences between Left and Right, conservative and liberal. For one thing, the Left is itself split on matters of philosophy as well as tactic and strategy. A review of the difference between Old and New Left may assist the reader in understanding the tensions existing in the leftist camp.

Although Lewis S. Feuer views the New Left/Old Left schism as part of a recurrent generational conflict, Armand L. Mauss feels that this is not the most useful way to regard the schism. A chronological generation is not necessarily coextensive with an ideological one.[10]

In order to understand the New Left, one must realize that its social origins are predominantly bourgeois rather than proletarian, and student or ex-student rather than worker. This has resulted in striking differences between the Old and the New Left regarding general orientation:

- The "manifest motivations" of the Old Left were economic self-interest and economic justice. The New Left, with its membership composed of students and ex-students reared in the upper middle class, is more interested in obtaining conditions of general social justice. Economic interests seem to have little to do with New Left activity.

- The Old Left took up the concerns of the working class, whereas the New Left has identified with the have-nots, drop-outs, ethnic minority groups, students, and inhabitants of the ghetto who remained poor even after the unions got a better deal for the worker. The political positions of the Old Left and the New Left differ in many ways:

- The New Left stresses individualism, whereas the Old Left stresses a need for collective action.
- The New Left is more reformist than Marxist, more present-oriented than future-oriented, less materialistic, less conscious of the need for security, and more predisposed to spontaneous change than to using contrived or parliamentary means for achieving change.
- The New Left is also less ideological and promotes the use of "people power" rather than "political power." Power is ideally decentralized according to New Left thought. The power of government is recognized as legitimate by the Old Left which is more prone to accepting an impartial, centralized bureaucratic welfare state.
- The New Left has been more concerned about dehumanization, racism, and indifference to poverty than about poverty as a fact and inequality or exploitation of the working class.
- One of the most striking differences among Leftists is the New Left's insistence on the need to cultivate man's individually unique characteristics, and the Old Left's seeming fear and intolerance of uniqueness which verges on becoming antisocial deviation.

These differences add up to a tremendous disagreement among Leftists concerning most educational issues.

When it comes to reforming the school curriculum, for instance, the Old Leftist is still adamant that there are certain core subjects which all students should be required to take. In these core subjects, students learn necessary skills and attitudes which prepare them to compete successfully in the economic system. Old Leftists believe that students should learn to contribute to the collective state rather than serve their own private interests. The New Leftist is equally adamant that the student has the right to choose his own preferred activities. The New Leftist is not usually concerned about the need to regulate or assimilate human beings in ways that oppose individualism.

New Left versus the Liberal Establishment. The showdown between liberal reformists and the archconservatives in educational circles was staged in the 1960s. Since then tensions have shifted to disagreements between the New Leftists and the "liberals" or "pseudo-liberals," who replaced the conservatives but did not basically change the institutions they promised to reform. Most radicals view most liberals in power as conservatives in disguise. The radicals seek to expose the pseudo-liberals for what they regard them as: that is, self-concerned bureaucrats who are accomplishing very little in democratizing the educational system.

It is sometimes interesting to trace the discussion of an educational issue across the spectrum of political thought from traditional Right to traditional Left, to the more liberal view and, from there, to the emphasis of the New Left. Take, for example, the differing opinions of educators regarding teaching the importance of collective action. The traditional Left thinks collective action and decisions regarding production are necessary in order to equalize the benefits of industrialization. The liberal may think collective action is necessary but only when it occurs as a result of democratic consensus. Liberals are sometimes opposed to the communistic leanings of the Old Left. In the New Left we find a new assertion of the rights of individuals to associate and innovate without interference. At the same time, the New Left believes in the importance of group spirit and group action if meaningful reform is to be realized.

The New Leftist is set off from the Establishment liberal in other ways as well:

- The liberal believes in the functional value of institutional structure. The New Leftist usually opposes any fixed structure, especially if that structure cements administrative procedure.

- The liberal is an equalitarian in many ways. The New Leftist is not so concerned about equal outcomes as he is about equalization of opportunity. What a person does with his opportunity is up to the individual.

- The liberal is regarded as a "homogenizer" of the community; he encourages cooperation and acceptance of a consensus. The New Leftist encourages diversity, emphasizing decentralization at the expense of bureaucracy.

- The liberal may attempt to reform institutions or policies which already exist. The New Leftist is usually pessimistic concerning the possibility of fundamental changes in existing institutions. The New Leftist therefore attempts to construct "counter" or "parallel" institutions which operate alongside the more traditional institutions.

- The liberal usually believes in contriving change through political means governed by majority opinion, whereas the New Leftist tends to emphasize the importance of group spirit and action in promoting change.

The value emphases in the student New Left are almost diametrically opposed to the value emphases of the dominant institutions established by corporate liberalism. The student New Leftists are usually utopian and idealistic. They may emphasize equality and freedom, but they do not stop there. The student Left shows disgust at affluence without merit, and consensus which does not regard people's practical need. Students today believe more in creative expression than in consensus and they desire to build a "countersociety" with flexible institutions that parallel the older, more rigid institutions in society. Consequently, the "free" and "community" school movements have been firmly launched by New Leftists while other radical educators such as Illich and Reimer have been more concerned with deschooling society.[11]

Traditional versus Nontraditional Educators. While continuing to consider the educator's response to student disaffection, let us examine the positions held by two theoretical groups whom we shall term "traditionalists" and "nontraditionalists." The assumptions of these two groups will be discussed primarily with respect to three areas: the function of the school system and its teachers, the nature of the student's role in the educational setting, and attitudes toward student dissent. (See Table 4.)

Table 4. Traditional versus Nontraditional Educators

Traditional Educators	*Nontraditional Educators*
Schools exist to preserve, extend and disseminate accurate knowledge.	Schools exist to facilitate the creation of a better environment.
The most knowledgeable members of a community are those who have the most experience. The most knowledgeable members of a community should control that community in order to preserve its defined function.	The teacher should be a human catalyst for learning. He does not necessarily have to be the most knowledgeable member of the community.
Resources are limited, so the school should restrict itself to the dissemination of knowledge.	Education does not necessarily have to take place in the school. Educational alternatives and community resources should be utilized in addition to the school.
The distinctions between administrators, teachers, and students should be maintained.	The distinctions between administrators, teachers and students should be reduced.
Schools should try to ensure the regular operation of society and not seriously threaten the existing power structure.	Schools should concern themselves with education even if it means threatening the existing power structures.
Schools should not concern themselves with extreme positions but should teach people how to accept society.	Schools should concern themselves with anything people want to know even if it threatens commonly accepted beliefs.

The traditionalist may believe, for instance, that "school exists to preserve, extend and disseminate accurate knowledge."[12] This belief assumes that most knowledgeable members of an educational community are those who have the most experience. It is also assumed that, by virtue of this knowledge, these members should largely control the environment in order to preserve its defined function. Traditionalists might argue that the most knowledgeable members of the educational setting are assumed logically to be the most appropriate teaching staff.

A traditionalist takes the stance that a school should use all necessary means to ensure the regular operation of society while trying to eliminate anything which could potentially lead to a shift in power, or seriously threaten the credibility of the existing control or power structure. While the notion of resorting to physical force is repugnant to many traditional educators, it is felt that if illegitimate force is used to interfere with the normal operations of an educational community, legitimate force must be used to combat it. It must be ensured that power does not fall into the hands of those who instigated the disruption.

Another assumption frequently made by traditional educators is that a school has at its disposal a limited amount of resources. Therefore it should be concerned only with the dissemination of strictly academic or occupational knowledge. This is not only to imply that the student's out-of-school or nonacademic activity is unimportant, but that the school's energy should be directed primarily to academic or occupational concerns.

Another traditional assumption deals with the nature of education. Education is not something that is done to people: it is something they do to themselves. On the basis of this assumption, complaints of irrelevant classes, poor teaching, and lack of meaningfulness are invalid. True education is a process of selection from within, not something inflicted externally.

From a traditional viewpoint, it is further felt that students are misled if they are taught that they can succeed in our society by adopting any other than the middle class, protestant ethic values. Disadvantaged minority groups *should not* therefore, be given special treatment within the system because such privilege would lead them into a false view of reality.

Traditionalists feel that any students who oppose or challenge the methods of the "most knowledgeable members" of an institution are wasting their time for two reasons:

● By virtue of their past experience and knowledge, teachers know what is important to learn and the best methods and environment for that learning to take place.

● Because students are only in a particular school for a limited time, and many of the teachers remain in the same school for years, students would not be around to feel the long-term effects of their proposed changes.

One academic goal of traditional educators is to establish an educational setting where accurate knowledge accumulated through historical experience is directed toward the maintenance of a stable, harmonious society. The more traditional faculty would hope to be in control of the system, although countenancing an appropriate degree of supplementary student decision-making power, thus assuring the system's ongoing harmony and the fulfilment of its ultimate function—the preservation, extension, and dissemination of accurate knowledge.

From the nontraditional perspective, the function of education is essentially "Getting to know, on all the manners which most concern us, the best which has been thought and said in the world; and through this knowledge, turning a stream of fresh, free thought upon our stock notions and habits" (Matthew Arnold as quoted by Louis Kampf).[13] Arnold does not see education as an end in itself, but rather as a means to facilitate the creation of a truly free educational environment.

It can be noted that both traditional and nontraditional factions are concerned with power:

- The traditionalist views ultimate control and power as an end in itself.
- The nontraditionalist may view power as a means to an end.

A second distinction can be made:

- The traditionalists view the educator as the "most knowledgeable member of a school system—a result of his past experience."
- To the nontraditionalist, the teacher's contribution is to be a human catalyst for students' intellectual and emotional growth.

With reference to the nature of the school system, the nontraditionals assume that the stress should not be placed on professionalism, but rather on development of individual natural talents and faculties, and that these should be developed at an individual pace and by individualized methods. Nontraditional educators claim that the present system rewards professionalism, and that professionals are overly concerned about their own social mobility.

Basic to the problem of inadequate communication between the Establishment and the student is the rigid distinction made between teacher and student. Kampf believes that the divisions between students, faculty, and administration have no place in any institution that claims to be primarily concerned with learning.[14]

Radical educators view the question of irrelevancy seriously. They state that industrialism has destroyed the natural environment, thus giving rise to real (indeed desperate) collective needs. Nontraditionalists believe that needs such as housing and community services cannot be met by the present sociopolitical structure because they contradict the profit motive upon which our society is based. Radicals believe that—

- students can see these pressing needs and are concerned;
- there are needs of society warranting *immediate* attention;
- distinctions such as "student" and "teacher" prevent collective action designed to fulfil serious societal needs.

Because human needs can no longer be met by the present sociopolitical system, radical educators see their aim as assisting in the development of a counterculture. They feel that loyalties to human life, rather than professionalism and national interest, are prerequisite to the attainment of this necessary alternative. "Many students are engaged in an almost frantic search for alternative careers and for alternative models of consumption—for a way of life in which production is subordinated to human needs, and activity is not simply geared to production."[15]

All educators have certain attitudes and perceptions concerning the nature of education, the function of the school system, the roles of student and teacher, and student dissent. Keeping these perspectives in mind, let us turn to an account of how these orientations manifest themselves in the behavior of those working in the secondary school system.

The administration of a secondary school is publicly responsible for dealing with any action taken by student radicals. Each administration is dictated to by two major factions, each packed with its individual vested interests: the parents of the students; and the political hierarchy above them, namely the board of education and the provincial department of education. To be free from either direct or indirect pressure from these factions, each administration must keep its school operating smoothly and without major disruption. Therefore when student dissent takes the form of physical action, the administration is compelled to attempt to reinstate some semblance of harmony and order as soon as possible. Even when a protest involves a small minority of the student population, the smooth functioning of the school is disrupted. The individual teachers are not *required* to act. The onus is on the administration. Even if a group of teachers did decide to act on some issue involved with student protest, any administrative action would take precedence. One must remember that the teacher in a school has a vested interest in retaining his job, and that any action straying too far from administrative policy may put his position in jeopardy.

Traditionalist teachers tend to stay behind the administration. They view any radical activity as disruptive. They feel the sooner the administration can disband the disruptive group the better, so as to return to the day-to-day educational routine which has been disturbed. The traditional teacher does not feel compelled to act.

Radicals sometimes state that any genuine student action should involve some initiative and organization on the part of the students concerned, and this without the formal supervision or direction of a teacher. It is a creative learning experience for the student to initiate and carry out a piece of action on his own.

The traditional educator is probably surprised by the protest and convinced of the unreasonableness of those protesting. If and when he must react to the protest, he does little more than deal with the immediate problem that has precipitated the protest. Such a response centres on specific issues and tends to look to a solution for the precipitating cause, without much direct consideration of long-term implications. One would also have to consider as traditional any approach that attempts to stifle, cut off, or muzzle protest. But many administrators have found that such responses only delay the day of showdown.

A more flexible educator is probably ready for some form of protest and willing to concede that those protesting may have reason. When protest occurs, and probably even before, a shrewd administrator will have already thought of alternatives to the existing procedures and policy. One way for the administrator to rationalize the use of alternative policies is to introduce them on an experimental basis. Dwight Allen says, "One way to unfreeze our educational situation is to legitimize experimentation. We could do this by writing legislation that would authorize school districts to set aside 10 to 15 percent of their present budgets for alternative schools, K–12, that would operate on a system of voluntary enrollment."[16] Allen suggests that such schools could become community laboratories of experimental education, and that, in time, they might perhaps undergird more extensive movements to renovate our educational system.

The answer to most protest should not be sudden or unplanned. An authoritarian is interested chiefly in quelling the protest. A man who suggests a program such as that of Allen is interested in understanding and then removing the major factors causing the protest. But in order to entertain such an approach to the problem, an educator must have reflected upon the entire educational system; he must also be willing to experiment and try to find viable alternatives to present procedures.

The nontraditional educator probably regards protest against the educational system as not only inevitable, but desirable. He understands and is in sympathy with the protesters because, like them, he disagrees with the basic assumptions of our present school system "about what is necessary, human, or good; the treatment of the person, time, choice, energy, work, community, and pleasure."[17]

Such a total rejection of the status quo permits of only one reaction, and Martin reflects the reaction of a revolutionary educator when he says that "those who want to help the young must realize it cannot happen in the schools."[18] He seems to be saying what Illich put even more directly and more positively: "I believe that the disestablishment of the school has become inevitable and that this end of an illusion should fill us with hope."[19]

Whereas the traditionalist questions neither the process nor the goal of the education process, the nontraditionalist is willing to question the process and the revolutionary questions and rejects both the process and the goal and would (though he may not) replace them with goals and methods which he feels are superior.

No response to student protest should be prepackaged, nor can a general pattern be applied to a particular problem. And what is more, the most effective method of dealing with protest may well be a procedure that inculcates elements of many past approaches. The team attempting to resolve the problems should be composed of people who represent each point of view. The contribution of each may be not only useful, but vital.

POSSIBILITIES FOR HUMANISTIC REFORM

Educators responsible for planning and reforming the schools of tomorrow need to be constantly reminded of the underlying reasons for student distress. Educational change should be systematically directed toward fundamental problems of the student if the presently dehumanized school system is to be remedied and improved. It may be helpful to outline some of the positive steps which must be considered while restructuring the educational system.

The crucial determinants of a student's development are the humanistic climate or atmosphere of the school and the student's sense of involvement in its program and purpose.[20] Tamminen and Miller report, on the basis of intensive researches on public schools, that the humanistic atmosphere of a school is one of the most important determinants of academic achievement and student satisfaction.

- These findings indicate that one thing educators must do in reducing the inhumanity of schools is to facilitate the creation of comfortable, stimulating learning atmospheres. In most schools students are not permitted to decorate and redecorate their schools and classrooms because school boards have regulations controlling the decoration of facilities. In a more humanistic school, one student task at the beginning of a school term would be to create a lively visual atmosphere. Visual stimulants such as posters, paintings, and collages could be used to enhance the school. Individual students should be encouraged to reflect their own beliefs and values through the personalization of some space of their own. On a desk or carrel might be imprinted emblems, monograms, or personal symbols. No rules should constrain the use or decoration of facilities beyond those rules deemed absolutely essential for purposes of safety.

- In the future, schools must be reduced in size, and school systems decentralized, if the humanistic environment is to be improved. The larger the school, the more impersonal and bureaucratic its atmosphere.[21] Tamminen and Miller found that only in small high schools was there any semblance of humanistic atmosphere.[22] The trend toward large, consolidated schools must cease if student alienation is to be overcome. D. H. Heath reports that many studies show a direct relationship between the increase in a school's size and decrease in student involvement in the activities of the school. Research is clear in indicating that, as a school grows, there is no proportionate increase in the number of extracurricular organizations.[23] In fact, students who are bussed to large schools from outlying areas frequently miss the extracurricular activities altogether. For this reason and many others it is essential that the trend to larger, central schools be discontinued and smaller regional schools be reinstated as the population increases. Those responsible for centralizing the school system have been more concerned with educating students to adjust to society than they have been with developing a society that is hospitable to the individual's real needs. Students need to be active and they need an opportunity to relate to their peers in their own ways and time. Until educators realize this, schools will continue to alienate the young.

- Educational planners should also concentrate on improving school staffing. A humanistic environment is partially facilitated by teachers and administrators who understand youth, who are not estranged from their own emotions, and who cherish openness and personal warmth in their interpersonal dealings. When the staff is brusque, controlling, competitive, and negative in its orientation toward students and teaching, the students suffer. Teachers must be freely themselves before they can become positive in their approach to students. Heath suggests that teachers abandon the role of playing "teacher" and learn how to be more fully human with students.[24] Nathaniel Hickerson, in his proposals for educational reform, emphasizes the need to produce a more humanistic breed of teacher in the future. He maintains that schools need teachers who understand children with economically deprived and varied cultural ethnic backgrounds. Improving the education of students with different backgrounds than our own is almost totally dependent upon our understanding of their particular problems.[25]

- Part of the improvement in teacher-student relations could be facilitated by the adoption of new definitions of the teacher's role in relation to students. Attempts should be made to make teachers see themselves as part of the classroom rather than as in control of it. Distinctions between the teacher as teacher and the student as student should be minimized. No superficial barriers such as dress or mannerisms should separate teachers from students. These distinctions and barriers have been all too frequent in maintaining distances between instructors and those they are commissioned to instruct. It is time that these distances be removed and that the teacher take his/her place among the students as an important but less conspicuous and authoritarian part of the teacher/learning process.

- Schools of the future need to be more open to the needs of all parts of the community. Schools of the past have served too long as remnants of a society which has passed. Needless barriers have been erected between the community and the school. Principals have accepted their role—defined by school boards—as filtering agents that serve to keep the school free from undesirable elements and influences that seek access to the student population. Perhaps the students need to be sheltered from certain kinds of people and information. However, there are many community agencies that should be making inputs into the school. The school should extend itself outward to the community. Instructors should have contacts in many relevant agencies, clubs, and organizations, and there should exist a constant flow of exchange between the school and the community. Parents should be welcomed at school. One aspect of community involvement could be school-promoted field trips of various sorts. Field trips could include overnight and weekday excursions. Education should take place off the premises of the school as well as in the school. Contacts with the community would increase the teachers' as well as the students' awareness of what is really happening in the world of work and keep them sensitive to the needs of society beyond the school.

- The school of the future should be marked by voluntarism. Teachers and students should be free to come and go to school as they please and little attention should be given to matters of attendance, truancy, and teachers who feel they need some free time. Many teachers have been made to feel irresponsible for leaving the school during a well-preserved free period. Releasing teachers in the future will be facilitated by maximizing the instructive resources within the classroom. Naturally gifted students should be encouraged to instruct other students. Particularly as student-teacher ratios continue to increase, teachers are going to have to look for alternative methods of instruction. Small group work guided by particularly gifted students is one way of humanizing the classroom as well as teaching new information and facilitating remedial work. The teaching profession has never emphasized the need to maximize teaching potential in a learning situation by using student help. Is there anything fundamentally undesirable about allowing knowledgeable students to temporarily replace the usual teacher? Encouraging the brighter students to teach the less bright would probably assist the development of compassion and human sensitivity. Perhaps it is time for the teaching of empathy to take priority over the production of top flight scholars, scientists, and Olympic athletes. Nothing should be done to discourage high performance and great proficiency, but slower and disadvantaged students should be given equal time and patience from the teacher and his/her assistants.

The principle of voluntarism in education acknowledges the fact that human beings learn much more efficiently when the motivation to learn is intrinsic rather than extrinsic. Creative voluntary association and innovation is desirable because it acknowledges the diversity of personality and interest within the school. Also when the student chooses his activity voluntarily, he has a proprietary interest in the completion of that activity. The time of forced participation and coercion by teachers in their attempts to make students comply with their expectations is definitely over. If voluntarism were the principle upon which schools operated, school subjects, in the formally understood sense, would probably disappear. Students would arrange themselves around instructors whom they regarded as being capable of offering them something worth while. An instructor, having full equality with everyone in school, could limit or open his class to as many or as few students as he desires. The instructor's responsibility would be to make known his general areas of proficiency as well as to tell the students how he/she might approach the task of teaching. Student choice in instructors would put pressure on teachers whose methods and manners were obsolete.

It would be impossible to describe, beforehand, the specific outline of an academic year spent in a school which was based entirely upon the principle of voluntarism. Calendars and course descriptions would probably disappear. No rigidification would occur as a result of overscheduling and predetermination of action. All transcripts would have to be prepared in retrospect. Each student would be involved in the process of evolving his own transcript. This is because students would postregister rather than preregister in all their courses. The chore of writing a transcript would be considered a task in creative writing.

REACTION TO RECOMMENDATIONS FOR HUMANISTIC REFORM

Those who resist the recommendations which have been suggested may do so for several reasons. Some educators feel that a "free" environment does not provide enough problem-solving discomfort. These objectors point to the importance of paradox in learning.

The advocates of free learning environments assert that they do not desire the removal of tension and conflict in the school. Rather, they wish to *reduce* "bureaucratic" tensions and *increase* the possibility of personal confrontation which results in more "creative" tensions. It may be argued that the kids don't see any tension as creative. A professor in a faculty of education asked, "How do you convey to people that you can have a tension-riddled environment without the loss of self-esteem?" My reply was that student insecurity is a matter to be treated with delicacy. If initial tensions are not too great and if, over time, students can be educated to cope with the fact that life involves the solving of difficult problems, this insecurity might be overcome.

It should be made clear that teaching highly disciplined activities, and evaluation through application of rigorous performance criteria should not be prohibited. However, behavioral objectives should be implemented only upon seeking permission of the student.

Other critics of the liberated school claim that its idealistic nature is insufficient to produce the qualities that a rigorous, competitive society demands. Students, they say, must be given a chance to consider not only their self-expectations but the expectations of others. Defence against this argument is provided by the fact that there would be representatives of other social groups present within the new open environment. Through community involvement and creative tension, students would be more than ever prepared to meet the demands of their society in later years.

One valid criticism of some free schools is that the students' free choice of activities may lead to drab overspecialization. Some educators argue that overspecialization begins earlier in the free school than in the traditional school. An example of how this happens is the fact that some students who fail math tests tend to leave math, and students who dislike French tend to quit language study. Proponents of the free school are frequently of the opinion that a person should specialize in the type of education that he likes best. That is, if a boy shows a predisposition toward building airplane models and none toward writing compositions, he should be allowed to engage in his model building and be encouraged to progress at his own pace. These proponents also feel that in the long run the boy's natural curiosity will lead him to expand his knowledge.

Critics of free schools state that the boy who wants to build models has been conditioned by his environment. If he is allowed to indulge in his preferred activity of building models for an indefinite period of time, he will fall behind in other important areas of educational development. Most educators seem to agree that, at some point in life, a person definitely has to commit himself to one area of study. But he should first come in touch with as much of life as possible, for it takes a strong spirit to catch up in a neglected area in later years. It is difficult for social scientists to gather enough appropriate data in order to make a decision as to whether the free schools are failing to develop an adequate cross section of interests in the students who attend them.

One positive consequence of the implementation of the reforms which have been suggested is that students of schools created with these reforms in mind may learn to be vigilant concerning their freedoms. Carl Rogers maintains that a person educated in freedom would eventually not tolerate an external environment that reduces his freedom.[26] Training persons to know the value of freedom is, in a sense, creating a society that would never submit to authoritarian control. Revolutionary movements led by free people would guarantee the removal of unfree or repressive elements. The resulting environment, according to Rogers, would allow the person to maximize in his human potentiality. The free environment also reduces negative effects caused by superficial and stigmatizing differentiation, labelling, and comparison. The negative effects of subservience, competition, conformity, compulsivity, false sequentiality, and unidimensionalism may be reduced as well.

SUMMARY

Whereas some educators have been encouraged by the students' insistence on having more responsibility and autonomy, other educators are alarmed. Educator response to student alienation, dissent, and confrontation seems to be regulated by deep-seated assumptions rooted in various ideologies and philosophies of the educator. Up until the sixties, conservative, rule-centred traditionalists seemed to have the upper hand in controlling the schools. Since then more liberal educators have taken the reins. Student radicals consider most of the liberals to have failed in that they dragged their heels on implementing needed reforms. Radical educators agree with the student protesters that the schools have far to go in the road toward liberation, relevance, and qualitative educational improvement. The liberals' use of terms such as "open," "progressive," and "innovative" (to describe new programs) has not convinced many educators that schools have fundamentally improved or even changed for the better since the 1950s.

NOTES

1. Kenneth Keniston, *The Uncommitted: Alienated Youth in American Society* (New York: Harcourt, Brace & World, 1965).

2. *Ibid.*

3. *Ibid.*

4. *Ibid.*

5. Bruce Joyce, "Curriculum and Humanistic Education," "Monolism vs. Pluralism," in *Humanistic Foundations of Education*, ed. Carl Weinberg (Englewood Cliffs, N.J.: Prentice-Hall, 1972).

6. Pierre Vallieres, *White Niggers of America*, Monthly Review Press, p. 60. Copyright © 1971 by Monthly Review Press. All rights reserved. By permission of the publisher.

7. Neil Postman and Charles Weingartner, *The Soft Revolution* (New York: Delacorte Press, 1971); and Soren Hansen and Jesper Jensen, with Wallace Roberts, *The Little Red Schoolbook* (New York: Pocket Books, 1971).

8. Postman and Weingartner, *The Soft Revolution*.

9. Gwynn Nettler, "Right and Left," a paper presented for broadcast on CKUA, Edmonton, Fall 1968. Excerpts printed with permission of the author.

10. Lewis S. Feuer, *The Conflict of Generations: The Character and Significance of Student Movements* (New York: Basic Books, 1969); and Armand L. Mauss, "The Lost Promise of Reconciliation: New Left vs. Old Left," *Journal of Social Issues* 27, no. 1 (1971): 1–20.

11. Ivan Illich, *Deschooling Society* (New York: Harper & Row, 1971); and Everett Reimer, *School Is Dead: Alternatives in Education* (New York: Doubleday, 1972).

12. T. F. Hoult, J. W. Hudson, and Albert J. Mayer, "On Keeping Our Cool in the Halls of Ivy," AAUP Bulletin 55 (June 1969): 186–91.

13. Louis Kampf, "The Radical Faculty," *The Humanist*, November-December 1969, p. 9. Excerpts reprinted by permission of the publisher.

14. Kampf, "The Radical Faculty," pp. 9–10.

15. *Ibid.*, p. 21.

16. Dwight W. Allen, "And How They Mangle the Young," *Psychology Today*, March 1971, p. 2.

17. Peter Marin, "Children of the Apocalypse," *Saturday Review,* September 1970, p. 72.

18. *Ibid.*

19. Illich, *Deschooling Society*, p. 44.

20. J. S. Coleman, *Equality of Educational Opportunity* (Washington: Office of Education, 1966); A. W. Tamminen and G. D. Miller, *Guidance Programs and Their Impact on Students*, Office of Education and Pupil Personnel Services Section, Minnesota Department of Education, 1968; and D. H. Heath, *Growing Up in College: Liberal Education and Maturity* (San Francisco: Jossey-Bass, 1968).

21. R. G. Barker and P. V. Gump, *Big School, Small School: High School Size and Student Behavior* (Palo Alto, Calif.: Stanford University

Press, 1964); A. W. Chickering, *Education and Identity* (San Francisco: Jossey-Bass, 1969); and Heath, *Growing Up in College*.
    22. Tamminen and Miller, *Guidance Programs and Their Impact*.
    23. D. H. Heath, *Humanizing Schools: New Directions, New Decisions* (New York: Hayden Book Co., 1971).
    24. *Ibid.*, p. 134.
    25. Nathaniel Hickerson, *Education for Alienation* (Englewood Cliffs, N.J.: Prentice-Hall, 1966), pp. 91–98.
    26. Carl Rogers, *Freedom to Learn: A View of What Education Might Become* (Columbus, Ohio: Merrill, 1969).

BIBLIOGRAPHY

Alinsky, Saul David. *Rules For Radicals.* New York: Random House, 1971.

Burton, Anthony. *The Horn and the Beanstalk: Problems and Possibilities in Canadian Education.* Toronto: Holt, Rinehart & Winston, 1972.

Cole, Stephen, and Hannelore Adamsons. "Determinants of Faculty Support for Student Demonstrations." *Sociology of Education*, Fall 1969, pp. 315–29.

Fairfield, Roy P., ed. *Humanistic Frontiers in American Education.* Toronto: Prentice-Hall, 1971.

Fish, Kenneth L. *Conflict and Dissent in the High School.* New York: Bruce Publishing Co., 1970.

Fisher, Robert J., and Wilfred R. Smith, eds. *Schools in an Age of Crisis.* Toronto: Van Nostrand Reinhold, 1972.

Goodman, Paul. *Compulsory Mis-Education.* New York: Horizon, 1964.

Greer, Mary, and Bonnie Rubinstein. *Will the Real Teacher Please Stand Up? A Primer in Humanistic Education.* Pacific Palisades, Calif.: Goodyear Publishing Co., 1972.

Gross, Beatrice and Ronald, eds. *Radical School Reform.* New York: Simon & Schuster, 1969.

Gross, Ronald, and Judith Murphy. *Revolution in the Schools.* New York: Harcourt, Brace & World, 1964.

Herndon, James. *How to Survive in Your Native Land.* New York: Simon & Schuster, 1971.

Hurwitz, Emanuel, and Robert Maidment, eds. *Criticism, Conflict, and Change: Readings in American Education.* Toronto: Dodd, Mead & Co., 1970.

Hurwitz, Emanuel, and Charles A. Tesconi. *Challenges to Education: Readings for Analysis of Major Issues.* Toronto: Dodd, Mead & Co., 1972.

Katz, Michael B. "The Present Moment in Educational Reform," *Harvard Educational Review* 41, no. 3 (August 1971) : 342–59.

King, Edmund J., ed. *The Teacher and the Needs of Society in Evolution.* Toronto: Pergamon Press, 1970.

Kohl, Herbert R. *The Open Classroom: A Practical Guide to a New Way of Teaching.* New York: The New York Review (distributed by Random), 1970.

Lurie, E. *How to Change the Schools: A Parents' Action Handbook on How to Fight the System.* New York: Random House, 1970.

MacDonald, W. Scott. *Battle in the Classroom: Innovations in Classroom Techniques.* Toronto: Intext Educational Publishers, 1971.

McGuigan, Gerald F. *Student Protest.* Toronto: Methuen, 1968.

Macpherson, C. B. "The Violent Society and the Liberal," *Canadian Association of University Teachers Bulletin* 17 (1970) : 7–15.

Ossenberg, Richard J. *Canadian Society: Pluralism, Change and Conflict.* Toronto: Prentice-Hall, 1971.

Postman, Neil, and Charles Weingartner. *Teaching as a Subversive Activity.* New York: Delacorte Press, 1969.

Sarason, Seymour B. *The Culture of the School and the Problem of Change.* Boston: Allyn & Bacon, 1971.

Taylor, Harold. "The Need for Radical Reform," *Saturday Review*, November 20, 1965.

Wasserman, Miriam. "School Mythology and the Education of Oppression," *This Magazine Is About Schools* 5, no. 3 (1971) : 23–36.

Wilson, R., and J. Gaff. "Student Voice—Faculty Response," *The Research Reporter* 4 (2), 1969.

*

Appendix: a new typology of student subcultures

STUDENT AND SOCIETAL subcultures are constantly changing in terms of values and focal modes of living out those values. There are several dimensions or variables upon which descriptions of subcultures can be based. After thinking about the material presented in this book, it may be useful to examine a new and tentative typology which includes more variables than the typology presented in Table 1. The purpose in presenting this new typology is merely to provoke creative thought and interpretation of the theoretical categorization of student behavior.

The figure in this Appendix illustrates the interactions of several sociopolitical variables. As we have seen, student thought and behavior ranges along a continuum from the political left to the political right. This differentiation is illustrated on the horizontal axis in the figure. Student behavior also varies in terms of its legitimacy under federal and provincial law and under regulations exclusive to the educational system itself. This differentiation is accounted for by the vertical axis. In Canada the traditional student subculture tends to the political right even though some so-called traditionalists may think and behave in a more leftist fashion. The alienated and radically political student subcultures tend to be leftist but also include a number of individuals who are rightist. The delinquent subculture tends to be more conservative and rightist but includes leftist revolutionaries of the nihilistic variety. One can see that each of these subcultures is represented continuously rather than dichotomously on each dimension. Similarly, the subculture labelled as the counterculture is superimposed upon the typology and ranges from one end of the vertical axis to the other. Any other subculture, such as the drug abuse subculture, could be superimposed upon the model and statistically validated through some sort of field research.

The tentative nature of such a typology must be emphasized. The idea is not to present a final or definitive typology with fixed boundaries or variables in mind. Rather, the idea is to stimulate interest and re-

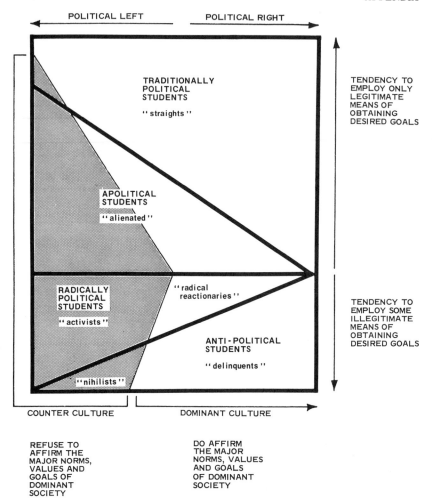

Subcultures in a Student Population

search in defining and comparing student subcultures. Naturally, those subcultures will continue to be transitional. It may be historically or sociologically interesting to examine proportional changes in the youth's subcultural identification from one time period to another. For instance, large numbers of radical student activists were in existence in the 1960s. The activist subculture may have decreased in members, and other subcultures may have grown in size since then. The typology, therefore, is interesting in that it allows comparisons at one point in time as well as comparisons over time. Some social scientists may be interested in testing the typology by attempting to test the incidence of involvement of students in each subculture at the present time or in the future.

Index

103